GREAT HOTELS OF THE WORLD: VOL.4
URBAN HOTEL
FROM ASIA TO EUROPE

PHOTOGRAPHY & TEXT
HIRO KISHIKAWA

SUPERVISION
SHINJIRO KIRISHIKI

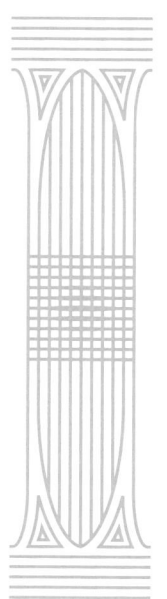
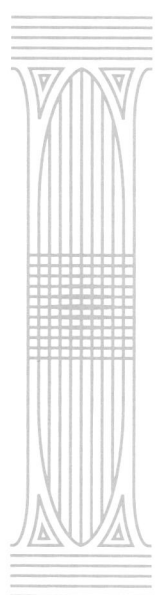
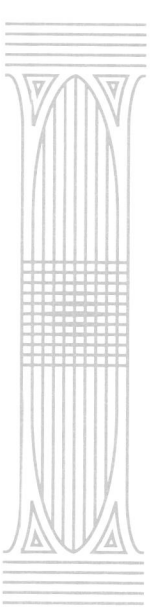

KAWADE SHOBO SHINSHA

序　桐敷真次郎 (建築史家・東京家政学院大学教授)

　この『世界のホテル』第4巻では、アジア、オセアニア、中東、北アフリカ、ヨーロッパの五つの地域の注目すべきアーバン・ホテルを取り扱う。取り上げられたホテルのうち、半数はいわゆるヨーロッパに属しているが、そのうちの三つはアテネ、ローマ、マラガ近傍という、いわゆる地中海文明圏に属し、もうひとつはビアリッツという大西洋に面するフランス南西部の著名な保養地にある。

　今日、地球を股にかけてビジネスにいそしむ銀行家やエグゼクティヴたちは、世界のいかなる地であろうと、会議と食事を楽しみ、第一級の設備と愉楽とサービスを要求する。もちろん、ホテル企業の側もこうした要求には敏感かつ精細に反応し、世界を結ぶ高級ホテルの連鎖網を着々と設営している。その結果、現在では世界のいずこでも、ほぼ同一水準の超一級ホテルを見いだすことができるようになった。そうした贅沢な顧客の増大に備えて、由緒のあるホテルは増築と改装と設備更新により、歴史の浅いホテルはまず最先端のデザインと多様な付属施設によって、それぞれこの新しい傾向に真剣に対処している。

　しかし、アメリカのアーバン・ホテルにもすでに見られたように、ポスト・モダンの時代にふさわしい新しいデラックス・ホテルに必要な微妙な配慮の要点は、時とともにより鮮明になっている。新旧要素の新鮮で巧妙な結合と混合がポスト・モダンの指標となっているのである。なぜなら、設備機器の耐用年数は建築に較べて著しく短く、それゆえ一定の歳月ごとにホテル建築には絶対に必要となるリノヴェーションが、もし単なる超高層化、単なる先端デザインの採用、最新設備の導入だけに終わるならば、それが必然的に世界の一級ホテルの均質化を招いて、顧客層のレベル低下をもたらすことが明らかだからである。多くの場合、歴史的様式の保存と地方的独自性の発揮から生まれてくるゆとりの価値が、これらのホテルの格式や風格の重要要素となり、特別の吸引力を形づくっていることが一見して明らかであろう。

　最近、世界一高価だった東京銀座のオフィス・店舗家賃がついに香港セントラルに抜かれたというニュースを耳にしたが、こうした香港の異常な隆盛は、1928年開業のザ・ペニンシュラ、1963年開業のマンダリン・オリエンタル、1980年開業のザ・リージェント、1991年開業のアイランド・シャングリラという、建物・サービスのいずれにおいても抜群の四つのホテルの展開に明瞭に見て取れる。香港は世界有数の過密都市で、超高層建築の林立する町であるが、香港の啓徳飛行場は九竜側にあり、航空機は町の上をスレスレにかすめて着陸するので、九竜サイドの建築は高さ制限がある。それゆえ九竜側にあるペニンシュラとリージェントは高層化しにくい。他方、香港島側は高層化の制限がほとんどなく、マンダリン・オリエンタルの25階、アイランド・シャングリラの56階という超高層化が可能となった。しかし、最も古い7階建のペニンシュラも、香港そのもののティー・ルームともいうべきその大ロビーの風格によって、いまなお人を魅惑してやまない。他の新ホテルは、当然中国的要素の導入でこれに対抗する。

シンガポールも狭い地域のなかでの急速な繁栄によって、建築の高層化が驚くほどのスピードで行われた町である。なかでもシャングリラ・ホテルは、スイート58を含む809室というアメリカ的な規模を達成し、しかも良好なサービスで好評を得ることに成功した。ザ・オリエンタルも、ポートマン設計の18階吹き抜きのアトリウムを売り物とするアメリカ型アーバン・ホテルの移植である。他方、ここシンガポールでは最古の名門ラッフルズ・ホテルが、サマセット・モームが顧客だった1920年代の姿に戻すという大胆な改修工事を行なっている。

　シドニーは、かつては古都メルボルンと盛名を競っていたが、著名なオペラハウスの建造以来、名実ともにオーストラリアの中心的近代都市となった。しかし、ホテル・インター・コンチネンタルでは、1849年建造の旧大蔵省という「歴史もの」を改装して、中庭をラウンジとする中心施設に変え、新たに31階建の超高層宿泊棟を組み合わせて、530室、42スイートの近代ホテルに変貌させた。

　ドバイ・インターナショナルは、1970年代のオイル・ダラーが生み出した中東近代ホテル群の代表的な一例で、15万平米の敷地に低層で354室という贅沢なレイアウトであるが、これは空港のごく近くに立地されているからである。荒涼とした砂漠的風土は、温帯からの旅行者には実に苛烈で衝撃的な感銘を与えるもので、このホテルも中庭、天幕、噴水といったオアシスのキャラバンサライのような趣向を加えて、憩いの場をつくりだすようにしている。

　同じ砂漠地帯でも、より文化的伝統の豊かなモロッコでは、マラケシュのラ・マムーニャ、フェズのパレ・ジャマイのいずれも、古いイスラム貴族の宮殿・邸宅を増改築して近代化したホテルであり、低層で室数も比較的少ないが、特異な伝統的装飾を魅力としている。モロッコに近いスペインのマラガ近傍のホテル・ビブロス・アンダルスでも、当然ムーア式装飾の内装が重要な特色となる。

　それゆえ、旧世界のヨーロッパに属するホテルの多くが、比較的小規模で、それぞれが何らかの建築様式上の特徴や歴史的由緒を誇りとしていることは格別不思議でない。唯一の例外は古都アテネのレドラ・マリオットで、これは、これまで近代ホテルが特に乏しかったアテネに投入されたホテル企業側の新しい拠点と見るべきであろう。しかしここでも、トルコ化によって貧しくなったギリシァの食事を一新するかもしれない異国風レストランの大胆な導入が注目される。

　イギリスのサリー州のセルスドン・パークは、一見アーバン・ホテルとは見えないお屋敷ホテルであるが、かつてのロンドン空港であったクロイドンに近く、また15室もの宴会場、18ホールのゴルフ・コースを備えている点で、やはりすでに掲げてきた最新の顧客の最新の要求に、きわめてイギリス的なやり方で巧みに応えていることがわかる。

Introduction by Shinjiro Kirishiki Architectural Historian and Professor of Tokyo Kasei Gakuin University

This book, Volume 4 in the series *Great Hotels of the World*, presents noteworthy urban hotels from five regions: Asia, Oceania, the Middle East, North Africa and Europe. Half the hotels included are located in Europe, but three of these (in Rome, Athens and near Malaga) fall more under the influence of Mediterranean civilization, while a fourth is located at Biarritz, a famous health resort in southwest France overlooking the Atlantic Ocean.

In recent years businessmen, bankers and others who travel the globe have come to demand first-class facilities, entertainment, food and service wherever in the world they go. Hotels have of course responded to these demands, and a network of top-class hotels has gradually spread throughout the world. As a result, wherever in the world one goes today one can find top-class hotels approaching the same high standards.

As we have already seen in the volume on American urban hotels, one requisite element in the new, deluxe hotels of the postmodern era has been a subtle, clever approach to the essentials of a hotel. In fact the fresh, skillfully executed fusion of the old and the new has become a hallmark of postmodern design and construction. Since the useful lifespan of a hotel's equipment and facilities is far shorter than that of its physical structure, all hotels must periodically close down for renovation work. If they merely install the most modern facilities, adopt the most extreme new design styles, and expand to the largest possible size, however, there will be an inevitable trend toward homogenization, and hotels will lose their individual character and attractiveness. To counter this, a great many hotels have developed their own personality and special appeal by taking advantage of unique characteristics, by preserving historical features or by drawing on local and regional styles and customs.

It was recently reported that Tokyo's Ginza area was finally overtaken by Hong Kong's Central district in charging the highest rents in the world for office and retail space. Hong Kong's enormous prosperity has been reflected in the extraordinary quartet of hotels covered here: The Peninsula, which opened in 1928; the Mandarin Oriental, open since 1963; The Regent, in business since 1980; and the new Island Shangri-La, open in 1991. Although Hong Kong, with its forests of skyscrapers, is famous as one of the world's most crowded cities, the height of buildings on the Kowloon side is limited by the nearby presence of Kai Tak International Airport and the countless planes skimming over the Kowloon rooftops as they land there. On the other hand there is practically no limit to building heights on the Hong Kong side, as can be seen by the 25-story Mandarin Oriental and the 56-story Island Shangri-La. However the oldest hotel, The Peninsula, standing at a mere seven stories, has maintained its charm through the years with its elegant grand lobby which has been called the 'Tearoom of Hong Kong.' Partly in reaction to this, The Peninsula's newer rivals have introduced distinctively Chinese elements in their design and facilities.

Singapore is another location where a rapid rise to prosperity has brought with it an extraordinary flurry of high-rise building. Among these new structures, the Shangri-La has not only achieved the size of a large-scale American hotel, with 809 guest rooms (including 58 suites), it has also earned an excellent reputation for its high level of service. Another new hotel is The Oriental. Built by developer John Portman with an 18-story central atrium, it is in many respects simply an American-style urban hotel transplanted to Asia. Countering this trend is Raffles Hotel, Singapore's oldest luxury hotel, which is currently undergoing a dramatic restoration project to return it to its original 1920s-era design, recalling the days when Somerset Maugham was one of the long-term hotel guests.

Although Sydney once competed for fame with the former Australian capital of Melbourne, ever since the construction of its famous Opera House Sydney has become, in name and in fact, Australia's foremost modern city. The builders of Sydney's Hotel Inter-Continental have restored a historic building, the 1849 Old Treasury Building, converted its courtyard into a central lounge and added a new 31-story guest room tower to create a modern, large-scale hotel with 530 rooms and 42 suites.

The Dubai International is typical of the modern hotels that sprang up throughout the Middle East after the sudden influx of 1970s oil money. The low-rise structures housing the 354 guest rooms sprawl luxuriously over a 150,000-square-meter site since the entire facility is built very close to the area's international airport. Although tourists coming from temperate zones may find the dessert landscape very fascinating but bleak, the overall plan mimics a traditional oasis resting place or caravansary, with fountains, tents and a central courtyard.

Elsewhere in the same dessert region, tradition-rich Morocco is the site of two hotels covered here, La Mamounia in Marrakech and Palais Jamai in Fez. Both were formerly palaces belonging to the local aristocracy, expanded and modernized when converted to hotel use. Both also feature low-rise construction, a relatively small number of rooms and charming traditional decor. Not far from Morocco, in the outskirts of Malaga in Spain, the Hotel Byblos Andaluz features Moorish-style interior decor as one of its drawing points.

It should come therefore as no surprise that many of the top hotels scattered through Europe—most of them relatively small in scale—often boast notable architectural features or points of historical interest. One exception is the Ledra Marriott in the ancient capital of Athens, which was specifically built in response to the lack of modern hotel facilities in that city; perhaps here the daring introduction of exotic foreign cuisine in the hotel's restaurants is an attempt to counter the standardization of Greek cooking which was brought about under the rule of the Ottoman Empire.

At first glance Selsdon Park in Surrey, England, may not seem to be an urban hotel—however its location near the former London airport in Croydon and its facilities, including 15 banquet rooms and an 18-hole golf course, show that the hotel is in fact simply responding to the demands of its mostly urban patrons in a thoroughly English manner.

GREAT HOTELS OF THE WORLD: VOL.4
URBAN HOTEL FROM ASIA TO EUROPE

Photography & Text:
Hiro Kishikawa

Supervision:
Shinjiro Kirishiki

Art Direction:
Toshihiko Kitazawa and Dix-House Inc.

Translation:
Robb Satterwhite

KAWADE SHOBO SHINSHA, Publishers, Tokyo.
2-32-2, Sendagaya, Shibuya-ku, Tokyo 151, Japan

Copyright © Kawade Shobo Shinsha Publishers Ltd., 1991
Photography and Text copyright © Hiro Kishikawa 1991

All rights reserved:
No part of this publication may be reproduced, stored in a retrieval
system, or transmitted, in any form or by any means including electronic,
mechanical, photocopying, recording etc.,
without permission of the copyright holder.

Printed in Japan by DAINIPPON PRINTING CO., LTD.

ISBN4-309-71584-2

TX
911.2
.K5358
1991

CONTENTS

2	序 INTRODUCTION by Shinjiro Kirishiki 桐敷真次郎		
8	The Peninsula, Hong Kong	Kowloon	Hong Kong
18	Mandarin Oriental, Hong Kong	Hong Kong Isl.	Hong Kong
28	The Regent Hong Kong	Kowloon	Hong Kong
38	Island Shangri-La Hong Kong	Hong Kong Isl.	Hong Kong
48	The Oriental, Shingapore	Singapore	Singapore
56	Shangri-La Hotel Singapore	Singapore	Singapore
62	Hotel Inter·Continental Sydney	Sydney	Australia
70	The Dubai International Hotel	Dubai	United Arab Emirates
76	Athens Ledra Marriott Hotel	Athens	Greece
82	Hotel La Mamounia	Marrakech	Morocco
92	Hotel Palais Jamai	Fez	Morocco
104	Hotel Byblos Andaluz	Mijas	Spain
114	Ambasciatori Palace Hotel	Rome	Italy
124	Hotel Metropole, Genève	Genève	Switzerland
132	Atlantic Hotel Kempinski Hamburg	Hamburg	Germany
138	Hotel Metropole, Brussels	Brussels	Belgium
146	Selsdon Park Hotel	Surrey	G. Britain
156	Hotel du Palais	Biarritz	France
170	Hotel du Louvre	Paris	France
178	Hotel Concorde Saint-Lazare	Paris	France
188	Hotels List		

The Peninsula, Hong Kong
Salisbury Road, Kowloon, Hong Kong

由緒ある歴史と優れたサービスでアジアのランド・マーク・ホテルと評価されているザ・ペニンシュラ・ホンコン。その建設プランは、1921年に開始され、1924年冬には開業する予定だった。しかし、ストライキやイギリス軍の駐留などで完成が大幅に遅れ、4年後の1928年12月11日にようやく開業。7階建、H型平面のホテルは、当時のカウルーン（九龍）地区最大の建造物であった。建築家は、このホテルの設計を最後に引退したW・D・グッドフェロー。

第2次大戦中の1942年には日本軍に接収され、「東亜ホテル」と改名された。大戦後の1945年9月3日、再び「ザ・ペニンシュラ・ホンコン」として営業を再開し、1978年には内部のリノヴェーションを終了。この時、大宴会場をレストランに改装した。現在、1992年完成予定の増設工事が進行中。香港の顔として世界中のリピーターを魅了してやまないホテルである。

●●●

With its long, distinguished history and its excellent level of service, The Peninsula, Hong Kong has earned a reputation as one of Asia's landmark hotels. Architect W.D. Goodfellow was responsible for the design, and construction began in 1923, with completion scheduled for the winter of 1924. Various problems, however, including labor strikes and occupation by the British army, delayed the opening until December 1928.

At the time of its completion this seven-story, H-shaped hotel was the largest building in Kowloon. In 1942 it was requisitioned by the Japanese army, and the name was changed to the East Asia Hotel. With the end of World War II it reopened to the public as The Peninsula, Hong Kong. Major renovation work was completed in 1978, and the grand banquet area was remodeled for use as a restaurant. The hotel is now being enlarged, and construction work is scheduled to be completed in 1992. Today, as throughout its history, The Peninsula continues to inspire the loyalty of its many regular patrons from around the world.

1-3：19世紀末から上海と香港で多くのホテルを経営した事業家エリス・カドゥーリのザ・ホンコン・アンド・シャンハイ・ホテルズ社（現在名ザ・ペニンシュラ・グループ）が開業したアジアの名門ホテル。1923年にJ・H・タガートを指揮者として建設を開始したが、さまざまな理由で開業までに5年を要した。4：開業時の姿をとどめる「ザ・ロビー」の天井。

●●●

1-3: This celebrated hotel was built by The Hong Kong and Shanghai Hotels Ltd. (now known as The Peninsula Group). The company was owned by businessman Ellis Kadoorie, and was responsible for the management of a number of hotels in Hong Kong and Shanghai. Construction began in 1923 under Managing Director James Harper Taggart, but for various reasons the hotel didn't open for another five years. 4: The original ceiling of *The Lobby*.

5

4-7: アフタヌーン・ティーがゆったりと楽しめる奥行約46mの「ザ・ロビー」。香港随一の優雅さと評される休憩スポットである。柱頭に"神"と"天使"の顔彫刻がつき、天井を神々のレリーフが飾る。ロビーには独特な16世紀イタリアの様式が取り入れられている。8:「ザ・ヴェランダ・バー」の入口部分。奥に同名の「ラウンジ」が設けられ、昼食(マルコ・ポーロ・ビュッフェ)も提供する。9: 英国エドワード朝風にリノヴェーションされたレストラン「ザ・ヴェランダ・グリル」。

4-7: *The Lobby*, 46 meters (152 feet) deep, serves a leisurely afternoon tea and has a reputation as being the most elegant place in Hong Kong to stop for a break. The lobby is decorated in 16th-century Italian style; faces of gods and angels are carved in the tops of the columns, and relief carvings of various gods adorn the ceiling. 8: The entrance to *The Verandah Bar*. At the back is *The Verandah Lounge*, and a buffet lunch (the "Marco Polo Buffet") is also served here. 9: *The Verandah Grill* restaurant was renovated in English Edwardian style.

6

7

10——The Peninsula, Hong Kong

8

9

Great Hotels of the World: vol.4 —— 11

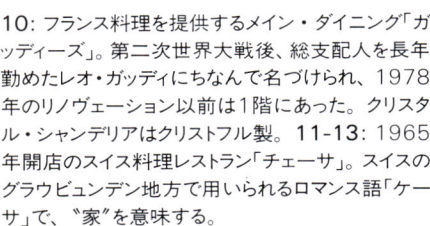

10 11

10: フランス料理を提供するメイン・ダイニング「ガッディーズ」。第二次世界大戦後、総支配人を長年勤めたレオ・ガッディにちなんで名づけられ、1978年のリノヴェーション以前は1階にあった。クリスタル・シャンデリアはクリストフル製。11-13: 1965年開店のスイス料理レストラン「チェーサ」。スイスのグラウビュンデン地方で用いられるロマンス語「ケーサ」で、"家"を意味する。

10: The main dining room, *Gaddi's*, is named after Leo Gaddi, who worked as the hotel's general manager after World War II. French cuisine is served. The crystal chandelier was made by Cristofle of Paris. The *Gaddi's* was on the first floor of the hotel before the 1978 renovation.
11–13: The Swiss restaurant, *Chesa*, has been open since 1965. The name means "house" in the Romansch language spoken in the Swiss region of Graubünden.

12 13

Great Hotels of the World: vol.4 ── 13

14

14-16: 広東料理を提供する「スプリング・ムーン・チャイニーズ・レストラン」。2階部分にプライヴェート・ルームがある。総面積約560m²。「ザ・ヴェランダ・グリル、ラウンジ、バー」と「スプリング・ムーン・チャイニーズ・レストラン」のインテリア・デザインはベント・セヴェリンが担当。また、ユニフォームは香港のファッション・デザイナー、エディ・ローのデザイン。17-20:「デラックス」と呼ばれるスタンダードの部屋。総面積約50m²。入口の壁とナイト・テーブルに取り付けられた表示パネルでカーテン、照明具、空調、テレビなどをコントロール。インテリアは19世紀の伝統的なフランスのデザインを模し、英国のチャールズ・ハモンド社が製作。浴室の床にはポルトガル産大理石が用いられ、シンク台が2個所設けられている。

14–16: *Spring Moon Chinese Restaurant* specializes in Cantonese cuisine. Private rooms are available on the second floor, and the total area is around 560 square meters (6,000 square feet). Designer Bent Severin was responsible for the interior of this restaurant as well as that of the *Verandah Grill, Lounge* and *Bar*. Staff uniforms were designed by Hong Kong clothing designer Eddie Lau. 17–20: A standard-sized *Deluxe* room is approximately 50 square meters (538 square feet). Control panels located on the night table and on the wall near the entrance operate the curtains, lights, air conditioning and television. The interior, done in typical 19th-century French style, is by the English firm of Charles Hammond Ltd. The bathroom is equipped with two separate sinks, and the floor is of Portuguese marble.

15

16

14——The Peninsula, Hong Kong

17

18

19

20

Great Hotels of the World: vol.4 — 15

21–25: 最高級の部屋「ザ・マルコ・ポーロ・スイート」。香港島を見渡す最上階に置かれ、応接間、会議室、主寝室、浴室（ジャクージ風呂付き）、客用寝室（浴室付き）、バトラーズ・パントリー（配膳室）、ゲスト用トイレなどで構成される。英国のマナー・ハウスを模したデザインで、応接間と会議室にはアンティークが飾られている。バトラー・サービス、ロールス・ロイスによる空港からの送迎が料金に含まれ、世界の王室に愛用されている最高級のスイートである。

21–25: The top-class *Marco Polo Suite* is located on the top floor and offers a commanding view of Hong Kong Island. The suite, designed to resemble an English manor house, includes a drawing room, meeting room, master bedroom, jacuzzi-equipped bathroom, guest bedroom (with separate bathroom), guest toilet and butler's pantry. The drawing room and meeting room are furnished with antiques. Guests staying in the suite are met at the airport and driven to the hotel in a Rolls Royce, and butler service is included. The suite is a popular stopping place for royalty from around the world.

16 —— The Peninsula, Hong Kong

23

24

25

Mandarin Oriental, Hong Kong
5 Connaught Road, Central, Hong Kong

香港島のビジネス街セントラル(中区)地区に、1963年9月開業した近代ホテル。25階建、長方形の建物は香港のレイ・アンド・オレンジ建築事務所の設計。インテリア・デザインは米国映画界のアート・ディレクターとして高名なドン・アシュトンが担当した。

開業以来、東洋的でかつ第一級のサービスを提供するホテルとして世界のエグゼクティブに愛好され、1987年には米国の〝トラヴェル・アンド・レジャー・マガジン〟により、世界のベスト・テン・ホテルのひとつに選ばれた。さらに1986年には米国の金融雑誌〝インスティテューショナル・インヴェスター〟のホテル・ランキングで第2位を獲得、現在も上位を保持している。1986～1988年にリノヴェーションが行なわれ、ホテル内部を一新した。1,100人の従業員が心暖まるサービスをしてくれるホテルとして名高い。

This modern hotel began operation in September 1963 in Hong Kong's business district, Central. The 25-story, rectangular building was designed by the Hong Kong architecture firm of Ray and Orange. Interior design was by Don Ashton, who became famous for his work as an art director for movies in America.

Since its opening the hotel has become popular with business travelers from around the world for its meticulous, Oriental-style service. In 1987 it was chosen as one of the world's ten best hotels by the American magazine *Travel and Leisure*, and in 1986 it was ranked number two by the banking magazine *Institutional Investor*, maintaining a high rank in the years since. Renovation work was performed from 1986–88, and the interior was modernized at that time. With its staff of 1,100 employees, the hotel has become famous for the high level of personal service it offers.

1-3: 547室のほとんどにヴェランダが付設されたホテルで、1986～88年のリノヴェーションでも再びドン・アシュトンがインテリア・デザインを担当した。4:最上階の25階に置かれた広東料理の「ザ・マン・ワー・レストラン」。本格的な古典広東料理を提供する。ファニチャー、窓飾り、天井をローズウッドで統一。奥に12席のプライヴェート・ダイニング・ルームがある。

1–3: Most of the 547 rooms are equipped with verandas. During the 1986–88 renovation work Don Ashton was once again responsible for interior design. 4: *The Man Wah Restaurant* on the top floor, serves authentic classical Cantonese cuisine. The furniture, window decorations and ceiling are all of rosewood. In the back is a private dining room seating twelve.

5
6

20——Mandarin Oriental, Hong Kong

5,6: 1987年にリノヴェーションを終えた「ザ・ロビー」。天井にクリスタル・シャンデリア、壁に黒大理石、床にはカラーラ産大理石が使われ、さらに中国絵画と古典的な黄金の大木彫パネル（約18m²）が壁面を飾る。階段を上った中二階には、アフタヌーン・ティーを楽しむ「ザ・クリッパー・ラウンジ」があり、キャビンを模した内装が取り入れられている。7: 入口正面の「レセプション」。左側に「問合わせデスク」、中央に「コンシェルジュ・デスク」、右側に「キャッシャー」。8:「ザ・コーヒー・ショップ」はカフェテリアの機能を持ち、一階に置かれ、外来者用の入口も設けられている。

5, 6: Renovation work on the *Lobby* was finished in 1987. Carrara marble covers the floors, black marble is used on the walls, and a large crystal chandelier hangs from the ceiling. The walls are also hung with Chinese paintings and large, classical-style gilt carved wood panels totaling 18 square meters (188 square feet) in area. Halfway up the staircase, on the second floor, guests can enjoy afternoon tea in *The Clipper Lounge*, which is fashioned to resemble the interior of a ship's cabin. 7: The *Reception* desk faces the entrance. To the left is the *Enquiry Desk*, at the center is the *Concierge Desk*, and to the right is the *Cashier*. 8: *The Coffee Shop*, on the first floor, offers cafeteria-style service and has a separate street entrance.

Great Hotels of the World: vol. 4 — 21

9

10

11

12

13

14

22———Mandarin Oriental, Hong Kong

15

16

9: 半地下階に置かれた「ザ・キャプテンズ・バー」。10: アジアを描きつづけた英国人画家ジョージ・チネリー (1774〜1852) の絵画が飾られる「ザ・チネリー・バー」。11, 12: 鉄格子のグリル台とビュッフェ・テーブルを取り入れた「ザ・マンダリン・グリル」の内部。13, 14: 宴会場の入口に置かれた彫刻と宴会場「コンノート・ルームズ」の中国絵画。15: 計5個所ある宴会場のひとつ「ウイロー・ルーム」。16: 24・25階の「ザ・ヘルス・センター」にはローマ風呂をイメージした室内プールがある。

●●●

9: *The Captain's Bar* is located on the basement mezzanine level. 10: *The Chinnery Bar* is filled with the works of George Chinnery (1774–1852), an English artist famous for his paintings of Asia. 11, 12: The grill and buffet table inside *The Mandarin Grill* are covered with iron latticework. 13, 14: A sculpture at the entrance to the banquet facilities, and a Chinese painting inside the *Connaught Rooms* Banquet area. 15: The *Willow Room*, one of the five banquet rooms. 16: The pool inside *The Health Center* on the 24th and 25th floor evokes images of a Roman baths.

17

17-19：九龍市街を見下す最上階にあるフランス料理のメイン・ダイニング「ザ・ピエロ」。入口にはメイン・ダイニングのバーとして機能する「ザ・ハーレクイン・バー」が置かれている。料理はクラシックなフランス料理が中心で、食器はナルミが使われている。
20-22：58室あるスイート・ルームのひとつ「ザ・タマール・スイート」。応接間、会議スペース、寝室、化粧スペース、浴室で構成されている。

17–19: The top-floor main dining room, *The Pierrot*, looks out over the shopping area of Kowloon. At the entrance is *The Harlequin Bar*. Classic French cuisine is the specialty, and the servingware is made by Narumi. 20–22: *The Tamar Suite*, one of 58 suites, includes drawing room, meeting area, bedroom, makeup area and bathroom.

18

19

24——Mandarin Oriental, Hong Kong

20

21

22

23-30: 近年リノヴェーションされた「ザ・マカオ・スイート」。玄関スペースがあり、右側に応接間、左側に寝室が独立して設けられている。応接間のキャビネット、寝室の天蓋ベッドなどを英国クラシック調にコーディネイト。浴室の壁と床には、青・白ピンクのポルトガル産大理石が使われている。なおすべてのスイート・ルームで、好みの石鹸を選べる"ソープ・サービス"が受けられる。

23-30: The recently renovated *Macau Suite*. The drawing room is located to the left of the entrance area, and the bedroom is to the right. The cabinets in the drawing room, canopied bed in the bedroom and other elements are coordinated in classical English style. The bathroom walls and floor are done in pale pink Portuguese marble. Each of the hotel's suites offers "soap service," allowing guests to choose their favorite soap.

26

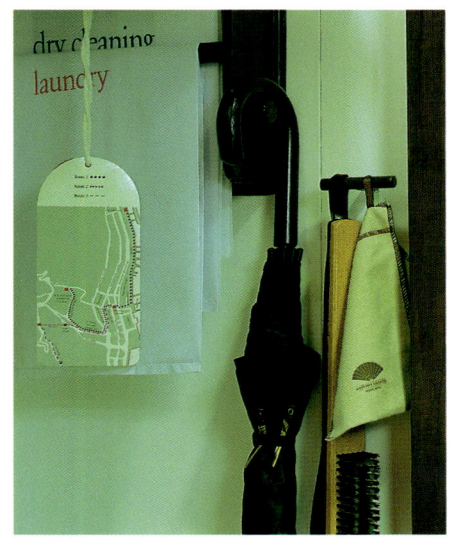
25

28

29

27
30

Great Hotels of the World: vol. 4

The Regent Hong Kong
Salisbury Road, Kowloon, Hong Kong

　ザ・リージェント・ホンコンは、カウルーン（九龍）地区のウォーター・フロントという絶好のロケーションを誇る。開業は1980年10月。17階建、赤い花崗岩で外装したホテルは、スキッドモア・オーイングス・アンド・メリル建築事務所とJ・チャンの共同設計。1984年には早くも米国の金融雑誌"インスティテューショナル・インヴェスター"によるホテル・ランキングで第5位を、87～88年には連続第2位を獲得し、世界の一級ホテルとして認知された。

　1986年から内部改装工事が開始され、まず最初に30室のスイート・ルームが改修された。最高級のデラックス・テラス・スイートは、広いテラスにジャクージ（泡風呂）が付設され、香港島の百万ドルの夜景を一望する素晴らしい部屋。現在も他の改装がゆっくりと進められている。現代の香港を代表する近代ホテルといえよう。

●●●

The Regent Hong Kong opened in October 1980 in an enviable waterfront location at the tip of Kowloon. The 17-story red granite building was designed as a joint project by Skidmore, Owings and Merrill and J. Chan. It is recognized as one of the world's top-class hotels; as early as 1984 the American banking magazine *Institutional Investor* ranked the hotel as fifth best in the world, and by 1987/88 it had climbed to number two.

In 1986 remodeling began on the hotel's 30 suites. Each of the two top-class *Deluxe Terrace Suites* features a large terrace with a jacuzzi and a "million dollar view" of nighttime Hong Kong Island. Remodeling work continues today at a gradual pace. This deluxe, modern hotel is often said to be representative of the modern Hong Kong.

1–3: 香港島から望む九龍半島の突端。左に旧九龍駅時計台、隣りに旧九龍駅跡に1980年オープンした「ホンコン・スペース・ミュージーアム」、右に「ザ・リージェント・ホンコン」。4: 屋根部分をリノヴェーションして、大きなテラスにジャクージを設けた「デラックス・テラス・スイート」。啓徳国際空港、ヴィクトリア・ハーバー、香港島の夜景を一望できる九龍唯一の場所である。

●●●

1–3: The tip of Kowloon Peninsula, as viewed from Hong Kong Island. To the left is the former Kowloon Railway Station clock tower, and next to it is the Hong Kong Space Museum, built in 1980. To the right is The Regent Hong Kong. 4: The roof portion was renovated and a jacuzzi was added to this *Deluxe Terrace Suite*. From its excellent vantage point it commands views of Kai Tak International Airport, Victoria Harbour and the nighttime lights of Hong Kong Island.

5

5-7: コーヒーショップ「ハーバーサイド」。朝6時から夜12時30分まで営業し、インターナショナルな料理を提供する。席数220。6: ドアー・マン。8-9: 香港島の景色を楽しむポピュラーなラウンジ「ザ・ロビー・ラウンジ」。朝食、ランチョン、アフタヌーン・ティー、カクテルなどが提供される。席数124。

5, 7: *Harbourside* coffee shop serves international cuisine. It is open from 6 a.m. to 12:30 a.m., and seats 220 diners. 6: A hotel doorman. 8, 9: *The Lobby Lounge* is a popular place to enjoy the view of Hong Kong Island. Breakfast, luncheon, afternoon tea and cocktails are served. There is seating for 124.

6

7

30 ——— The Regent Hong Kong

8

9

Great Hotels of the World: vol. 4 —— 31

10

13

14

11

15

12

16

10-12,16：夜7時から開店するレストラン「プルーム」は革新的ヨーロッパ料理を提供。17・18世紀の中国美術と磨き上げた黒大理石で装飾された二層にわたるレストラン。ワイン・セラーに8,000本のワインを貯蔵。席数160。13-15：「ロビー」中2階に位置するバー「ザ・メザニーン・ラウンジ」とトイレの表示。17-19：ビジネス・エグゼクティブに好評のブレックファスト・ミーティングが朝7時から可能な「ザ・ステーキ・ハウス」。昼と夜はアメリカ牛、シーフード、サラダ・バーが楽しめる。

●●●

10-12, 16: *Plume* restaurant, open from 7 p.m., specializes in innovative European cuisine. This two-level restaurant seats 160 and features 17th- and 18th-century Chinese artwork and black polished marble. The wine cellar contains some 8,000 bottles of wine. **13-15:** *The Mezzanine Lounge*, a bar located on the mezzanine floor of the lobby, and a rest room sign. **17-19:** Breakfast meetings, popular with visiting businessmen, begin at 7 a.m. in *The Steak House*. At lunch and dinner guests can enjoy American beef, seafood and a salad bar.

32——The Regent Hong Kong

17

18

19

20

20: 伝統的な広東料理のレストラン「ライ・チン・ヒーン」。ここでは〝飲茶(ヤムチャ)〟も楽しめる。席数118。21: 香港のホテルで最大の面積をもつ屋外プール。下部に「ヘルス・スパ」が設けられている。22-24: 70室あるスイートのひとつ「パティオ・スイート」。ホテルのすべてのゲストに、チェック・イン時にフルーツと中国茶のサービスがある。2種類の新聞とミネラル・ウォーターのサービスも料金に含まれている。

20: *Lai Ching Heen* restaurant serves typical Cantonese cuisine as well as *dim sum*. The restaurant accommodates 118. 21: The largest pool of any Hong Kong hotel is located next to the *Health Spa*. 22–24: The *Patio Suite* is one of 70 suites. All hotel guests are served fresh fruit and Chinese tea when they check in, and two daily newspapers and mineral water are provided complimentary.

21

22

23
24

25-27: 2つある「デラックス・テラス・スイート」。香港島の大パノラマを楽しめるように大テラスにジャクージまで設けた究極のスイート。応接間、2つの寝室、2つの浴室から成り、2層にわたっている。目的により他の部屋ともコネクトできる設計。インテリア・デザインはドン・シェムビエダが担当した。

25–27: Each of the two *Deluxe Terrace Suites* includes a jacuzzi on the large terrace from which to enjoy the magnificent view of Hong Kong Island. Each suite includes a drawing room, two bedrooms and two bathrooms, extending over two floors. Additional rooms may also be connected, depending on the guests' requirements. Don Siembieda was responsible for the hotel's interior design.

25

26

27

Island Shangri-La Hong Kong

Pacific Place, 88 Queensway, Central, Hong Kong

　1990〜91年、香港島のセントラル（中区）地区に開発された商業ビル群がパシフイック・プレイスである。三つの高層ビルにホテルを設け、マンションやオフィス・スペースも付加、さらに下層（1〜4階）をショッピング・コンプレックスで結んだ。このパシフイック・プレイス西側の56階建のビルに設けられたのがアイランド・シャングリラ・ホンコンで、開業は1991年3月1日。設計はウォン・アンド・オーヤン社。インテリア・デザインはリース・ロバートソン・フリーマン・デザイナーズ社が担当した。

　5〜7階にレセプションと飲食施設、8〜38階にオフィス、最上部39〜56階のアトリウム周囲に客室が設けられ、アトリウムを飾る中国画は中国本土の景勝地を描いた巨大なもの。最上部のレストランとラウンジは、九龍全域を眺望する人気のレストランとなっている。

●●●

　Pacific Place, a new commercial complex in Hong Kong Island's Central District, was completed in 1990–91. Three high-rise buildings contain a mix of hotel facilities, office space and residential units, and are attached to a low-rise shopping complex. The Island Shangri-La Hong Kong occupies part of the 56-story building on the western side of the complex.

　The hotel, which opened in March 1991, was designed by the firm of Wong & Ouyang (HK), with interior design by Leese Robertson Freeman Designers Limited. The reception area and dining facilities are on the fifth through seventh floors, and guest rooms are on the 39th through 56th floors at the top of the building, around a central atrium space. (Offices occupy the 8th through 38th floors). The atrium space features a gigantic, 14-story Chinese landscape painting. The restaurant and lounge at the very top of the hotel are the first public facilities to offer such an expansive view of the entire Kowloon region, and they have become enormously popular.

1, 2: ヴィクトリア・ピークから望む香港島市街。左上方に九龍半島、ヴィクトリア・ハーバーをはさんで手前が香港島セントラル地区。中央右寄りに建設中の楕円形ホテルが見える。3: パリのホテル・リッツで総支配人を務めたディディエ・D・ピコー氏がこのホテルの総支配人。4: イタリア産カラーラ大理石の床、径5mのオーストリア製クリスタル・シャンデリア、階段の中国絵画など、東洋と西洋の意匠を融合した「ロビー」。

●●●

1, 2: The streets of Hong Kong Island, seen from Victoria Peak. To the upper left are Kowloon Peninsula and Victoria Harbour, and in the lower portion of the photo is Central District. Just to the right of the center, the ellipseshaped hotel can be seen under construction. 3: General Manager Didier D. Picquot was formerly the General Manager of the Hotel Ritz in Paris. 4: The *Lobby*, with its Italian Carrara marble floors, 5-meter (16-foot) Austrian crystal chandelier and Chinese panel paintings, combines design elements from the Orient and the West.

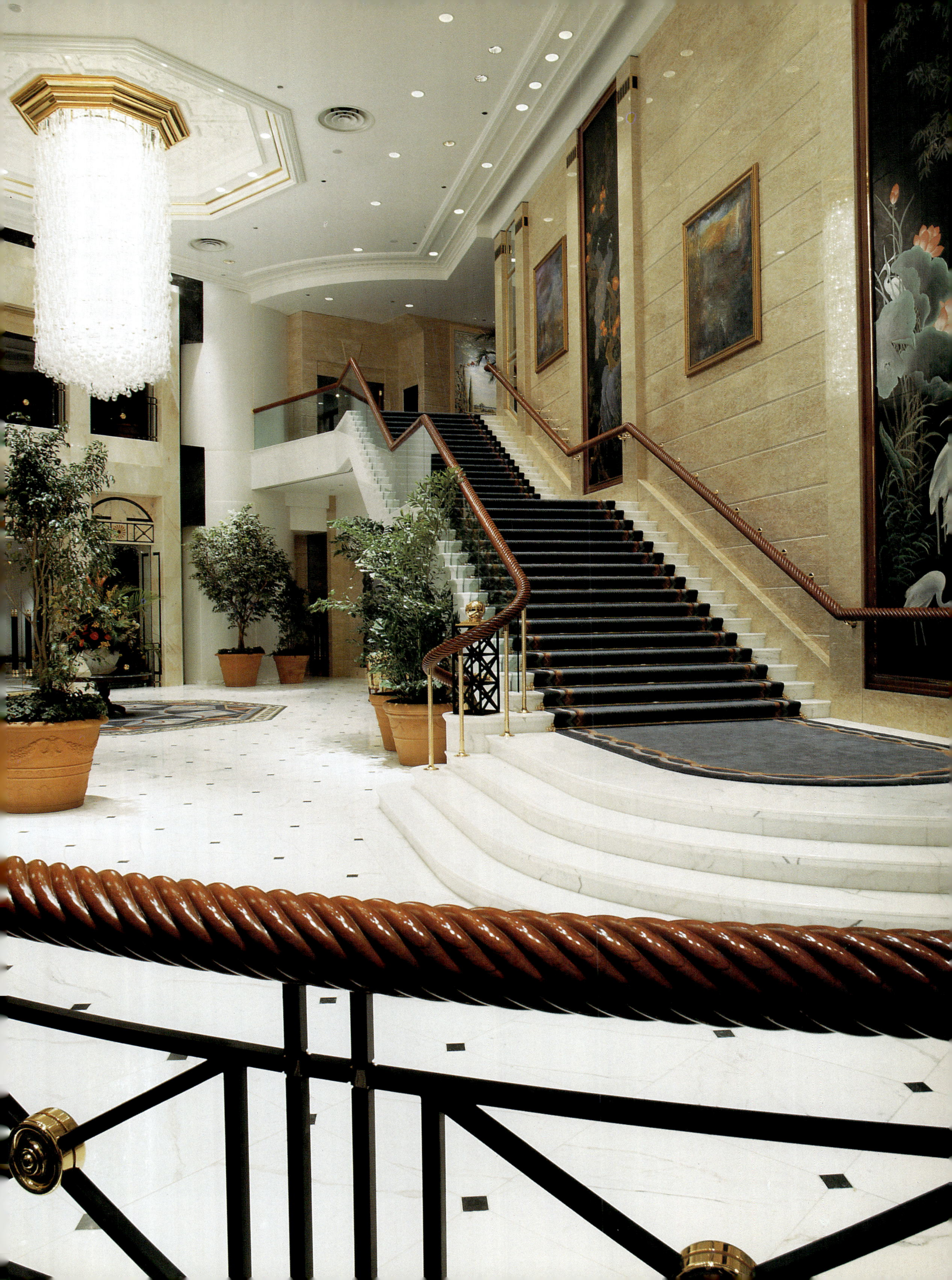

40 —— Island Shangri-La Hong Kong

9
10

5,6: 楕円形の建物の形をそのまま取り込んだ「レセプション」。ここに「コンシェルジュ」や「キャッシャー」のブースが置かれている。7,8: 入口正面の「ゲスト・リレーション・デスク」で客を各室へ案内し、客室でチェック・インのレジストレーションが行なわれる。9: カクテルや英国式アフタヌーン・ティーを楽しめる「ロビー・ラウンジ」。ティー・カップは特注のジノリ焼が使われている。10: ねじり柱のうしろに「ゲスト・リレーション・デスク」がある。右手が「メイン・エントランス」中央奥が「ロビー・ラウンジ」。

●●●●

5, 6: The *Reception* area reflects the overall shape of the building. The *Concierge* and *Cashier* desks are located here. 7, 8: From the *Guest Relations Desk*, facing the entrance, guests are shown to their rooms, where check-in procedures are completed. 9: The *Lobby Lounge* serves cocktails and an English-style afternoon tea. The teacups were specially made by Richard Ginori. 10: Behind the spiral column is the *Guest Relations Desk*. The main entrance is to the right, and the *Lobby Lounge* is to the rear of the center.

11–13:「ロビー」を見下す会議室を持つ「ビジネス・センター」。秘書サービスなどが受けられる。 14: シーフードを主体とした料理を提供する「ロブスター・バー」。英国調のインテリアで飾られ、常時新鮮なロブスターが味わえる。 15–18: ドア・パネル、スクリーン、カーペットを〝4つの花びら〟でデザインし、北京の〝夏の離宮〟を模した広東料理のレストラン「サマー・パレス」。ヴェネチア製のクリスタル・シャンデリアで飾られ、食器は日本のナルミが使われている。

●●●

11–13: The *Business Center* provides secretarial service, and has a meeting room overlooking the *Lobby*. 14: The *Lobster Bar* features an English-style interior. It specializes in seafood, including fresh lobster. 15–18: The *Summer Palace* Cantonese restaurant is modeled after the summer palace in Beijing. A four-petal flower motif unifies the design of the door panels, screens and carpets. The crystal chandeliers were made in Venice, and the place settings are Narumi bone china from Japan.

15
16
17
18

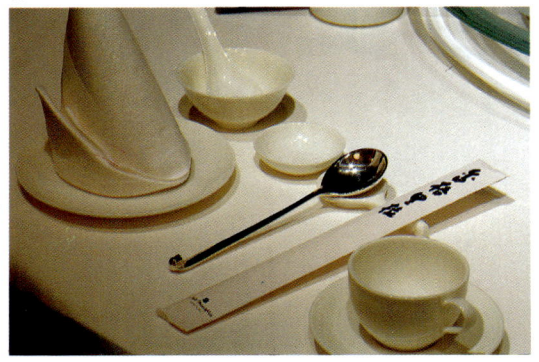

Great Hotels of the World: vol.4 — 43

44 ——— Island Shangri-La Hong Kong

21

22

23

24

25

26

19: カリフォルニア・スタイルのカジュアル・レストラン「アイランド・カフェ」。20: バンケット形式で500人、レセプション形式で1,000人の収容能力を持つ「グランド・ボールルーム」。クリスタル・シャンデリアはオーストリアのE・バカロヴィッツ製。このホテルを飾るために計1,000個の特製クリスタル・シャンデリアが作られた。21,22: 大壁画を飾った56階の眺望レストラン「ペトリュス」。ミュージック・ラウンジ「シラノ」もこの階にある。23: パブリック・スペースの壁を飾る照明具と絵画。24: 日本料理店「なだ万」。25,26: 特製のケーキとチョコレートが楽しめるデリカテッセン「ジ・アイランド・グルメ」。

19: The *Island Cafe* is a California-style casual restaurant. 20: The *Grand Ballroom* has a capacity of 500 guests for banquet-style events, or 1,000 persons for receptions. The crystal chandeliers were made by E. Bakalowits of Vienna. A total of 1,000 specially made crystal chandeliers are used in the hotel. 21, 22: Large murals cover the walls of *Petrus* restaurant. Guests can enjoy a panoramic view from the 56th floor while dining. *Cyrano* music lounge is also located on this floor. 23: Lighting fixtures and paintings in one of the public areas. 24: *Nadaman* Japanese restaurant. 25, 26: The *Island Gourmet* delicatessen serves specially made chocolates and cake.

27-29: 39～56階のアトリウムを飾る山水画は14階分（51m×13m）を占める巨大さで、北京工芸美術研究所の30名の画家により描かれた。素材はシルクを裏地とした中国紙250枚で、チベット、万里の長城、黄河、北京などが描かれている。**30:** エレベーターの待合いスペースもコリドールの雰囲気に仕上げられている。**31-34:** 44㎡という広いスペースを持つスタンダードの「ハーバー・ビュー・ルーム」。部屋には天井蛇腹、クリスタル・シャンデリアが付けられ、電気ティー・ポットも置かれている。浴室にはポルトガル産大理石が用いられ、シャワー・ブースやビデも付設。このホテルには34室の「スィート・ルーム」が用意されている。

27-29: A gigantic, 14-story Chinese watercolor painting hangs in the atrium space between the 39th and 56th floors. The painting is 51 meters by 13 meters (167 ft.×43 ft.) in size, and is made from 250 separate panels of silk-backed Chinese painting paper. It was painted by 30 artists from the Beijing Arts and Crafts Research Institute, and depicts the landscape of Tibet, the Yellow River and the Great Wall of China. **30:** The designers have sought to create a pleasant atmosphere even in the corridors and elevator waiting areas. **31-34:** A standard *Harbour View Room* has an area of 44 square meters (474 sq. ft.), and includes crystal chandeliers and a corniced ceiling. An electric teapot is provided in each room, and bathrooms are covered in Portuguese marble and equipped with shower stalls and bidets. The hotel also offers 34 suites.

31

32

33

34

Great Hotels of the World: vol. 4 —— 47

The Oriental, Shingapore
5 Raffles Avenue, Marina Square, Singapore 0103

　1987年、9万m²を誇るシンガポールの新しい埋め立て地に、3つのホテルを地下のショッピング・コンプレックス（250店舗）で結ぶホテル都市「マリーナ・スクエア」が誕生した。

　三つのホテルとはザ・マリーナ・マンダリン（22階建、640室）、ザ・パン・パシフィック・シンガポール（37階建、850室）、ザ・オリエンタル・シンガポール（21階建、515室）で、いずれも"アトリウムの魔術師"といわれる建築家兼デヴェロッパーのジョン・ポートマンの設計。

　ザ・オリエンタル・シンガポールの開業は1987年2月。18階分を吹き抜いたアトリウムには、ホテルのマークである扇形のデザインが取り入れられた。開業間もないホテルでありながら、早くもシンガポールを代表する優良ホテルと評価されている。またマリーナ・スクエアは、80年代の新しいホテル都市の開発としてホテル建築史に名を残すこととなるだろう。

●●●

　In 1987 Marina Square, a new "hotel city" with three hotels and a connecting 250-store underground shopping complex, was developed on 92,000 square meters (23 acres) of reclaimed land. Marina Square's hotels are The Marina Mandarin (22 stories, 640 rooms); The Pan Pacific Singapore (37 stories, 850 rooms); and The Oriental, Singapore (21 stories, 515 rooms). All three were built by American Architect and developer John Portman, sometimes called the "Wizard of Atriums."

　The Oriental opened in February 1987. It features an 18-story atrium in the shape of a folding fan, which is also the hotel's logo. Although only recently completed, the hotel has already earned a reputation as one of Singapore's best hotels, and the opening of the Marina Square "hotel city" was a major event in the history of 1980's hotel development.

1,2: L字形と半円錐形の建物が組み合わされた形のホテルである。半円錐形の建物上部に最高級の2つのスイート、「プレジデンシャル・スイート」と「マリーナ・スイート」がある。3: 送迎車のドアに付けられたホテルの扇形のロゴ。4,5: 半円錐形建物の内部では、マークの扇形を取り入れたユニークなアトリウムが18階分を吹き抜いている。

●●●

1, 2: The hotel comprises an L-shaped building and a semi-conical building. At the top of the semi-conical section are two of the hotel's top-class suites, the *Presidential Suite* and *Marina Suite*. 3: The hotel's fan-shaped logo appears on the car used for pickup service. 4, 5: Inside the semi-conical portion is an unusual 18-story atrium in the shape of a folding fan.

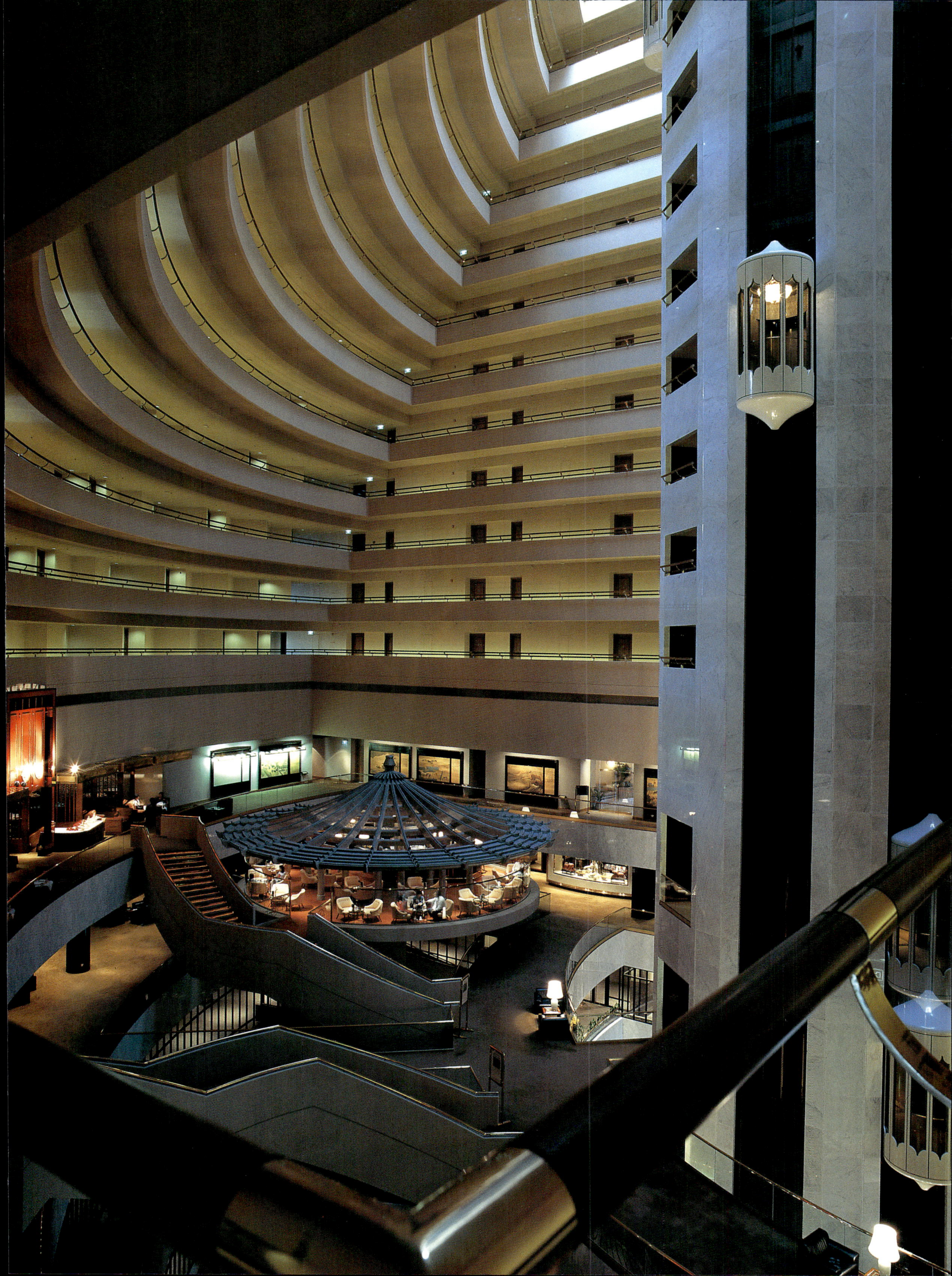

5
6

7

6: アトリウム5階の「アペリティフ・バー」。アフタヌーン・ティーも楽しめる。写真中央奥の円型屋根は4階につくられた「アトリウム・ラウンジ」。アトリウムの階段を降りた地下2層に、250の店舗、4つのデパート、映画館、2,500台収容の駐車場から成る総面積約59,000㎡のショッピング・コンプレックスが造られている。7: レストラン「カフェ・パーム」。8,9: 歴史に名を残した世界のキャプテンたちの肖像画で飾られた「キャプテンズ・バー」。

6: *L'Aperitif Bar*, on the atrium's fifth floor, also serves afternoon tea. Near the center of the photo is the circular-roofed *Atrium Lounge* on the fourth floor. Downstairs from the atrium is a two-level shopping complex of 250 stores, four department stores, a movie theater and parking for 2,500 cars, with a total area of 59,000 square meters (635,000 sq. ft.). 7: The restaurant *Cafe Palm*. 8, 9: Portraits of the world's famous captains from history line the walls of the *Captain's Bar*.

8

9

Great Hotels of the World: vol. 4

52 —— The Oriental, Shingapore

12

13

14

15

10: グリル台とワイン・セラーを入口に配したコンチネンタル料理のレストラン「フォーシェッツ」。11: 明朝の貴族邸宅の中庭を模した中国料理のレストラン「ザ・チェリー・ガーデン」。このホテルのレストラン、ラウンジ、宴会場のデザインはインテリア・デザイナーのドン・アシュトンによる。12,13: 白を基調としたトロピカルな「ヘロン・スイート」。「ウエルカム・ティー・サービス」は全室で受けられる。14,15: 中国調にインテリア・コーディネイトされた「パイ・シン・スイート」。

● ● ●

10: A grill and wine cellar are situated near the entrance to *Fourchettes* Continental restaurant. 11: The design of *The Cherry Garden* Chinese restaurant incorporates a replica of a Ming Dynasty nobleman's courtyard. Interior design for the restaurants, lounges and banquet areas is the work of Don Ashton. 12, 13: The tropical *Heron Suite* is decorated mainly in white. Guests in all room receive "Welcome Tea Service." 14, 15: The Chinese-style interior of the *Pai Shin Suite*.

54 —— The Oriental, Shingapore

19

20

16-20: 2つ置かれている最高級の部屋のひとつ「マリーナ・スイート」は二層にわたるデュプレックス式。応接間、読書室、会議室、主寝室、浴室、客寝室（浴室つき）、化粧室、大きなヴェランダから構成され、螺旋階段など、船内をイメージさせるデザイン。主寝室の浴室には黒御影石を使い、大きなワードローブを備えている。

●●●

16–20: The duplex *Marina Suite* is one of two-class suites available. The interior design, incorporating a spiral staircase and other elements, creates the impression of being onboard a ship. The suite includes a drawing room, library, meeting room, master bedroom, bathroom, guest bedroom (with bath), powder room and a large veranda. The master bathroom is done in black granite, and includes a large wardrobe.

Shangri-La Hotel Singapore
Orange Grove Road, Singapore 1025

　1971年の開業以来、シンガポールの美しい庭園ホテルとして親しまれてきたのがシャングリラ・ホテル。「シャングリラ」とは「桃源郷」の意である。5万m²の庭園には、大プール、ミニ・ゴルフ場、テニス・コートなどがあり、メイン・ビルディング(旧館)とガーデン・ウイング(1978年オープン)の二つの宿泊棟があった。1985年6月、新たに17階建、136室から構成されたデラックスなヴァリー・ウイングが開業した。ヴァリー・ウイングは、個人客のプライバシーを保護する配慮から開発された特別のウイングで、地下にヘルス・クラブがあり、宿泊客専用のレセプションが置かれ、専用のスカイ・ブリッジで飲食施設に結ばれている。

　シャングリラは、米国の金融雑誌〝インスティテューショナル・インヴェスター〟のホテル・ランキングで常に上位にランクされるアーバン・リゾート・ホテルである。

　Since it opened in 1971 the Shangri-La has become well known for its beautiful gardens. A large pool, tennis courts and a miniature golf range are contained within the 50,000 square meter (12.3 acre) gardens. There are three guest room wings: the original Main Building: the newer Garden Wing, which opened in 1978; and the deluxe Valley Wing. The 17-story Valley Wing opened in June 1985 and has 136 guest rooms. The hotel staff carefully protects the privacy of guests staying in this special wing, and facilities include an underground health club, a reception area exclusively for the guests, and a connecting sky bridge with dining facilities.

　The Shangri-La is an urban resort hotel that has earned an excellent reputation around the world, and it is ranked highly by the American banking magazine *Institutional Investor*.

1: 112室の部屋、24室のスイートを有する「ヴァリー・ウイング」。宿泊者専用の車用入口が設けられている。2: ホテルの全景。左側が「ヴァリー・ウイング」、中央が「メイン・ビルディング」(512室)、そして右側が「ガーデン・ウイング」(161室)。3:「レセプション」には、「ゲスト・リレーション」係が常駐し、「コンシェルジュ」の役割を担っている。4:「ヴァリー・ウイング」の「ロビー」。

1: The Valley Wing has 112 individual rooms and 24 suites, and provides a car entrance exclusively for guests. **2:** An overview of the hotel. To the left is the Valley Wing, in the center is the Main Building (with 512 rooms), and to the right is the Garden Wing (with 161 rooms). **3:** The *Guest Relations Desk* in the reception area is responsible for concierge services. **4:** The *Lobby* of the Valley Wing.

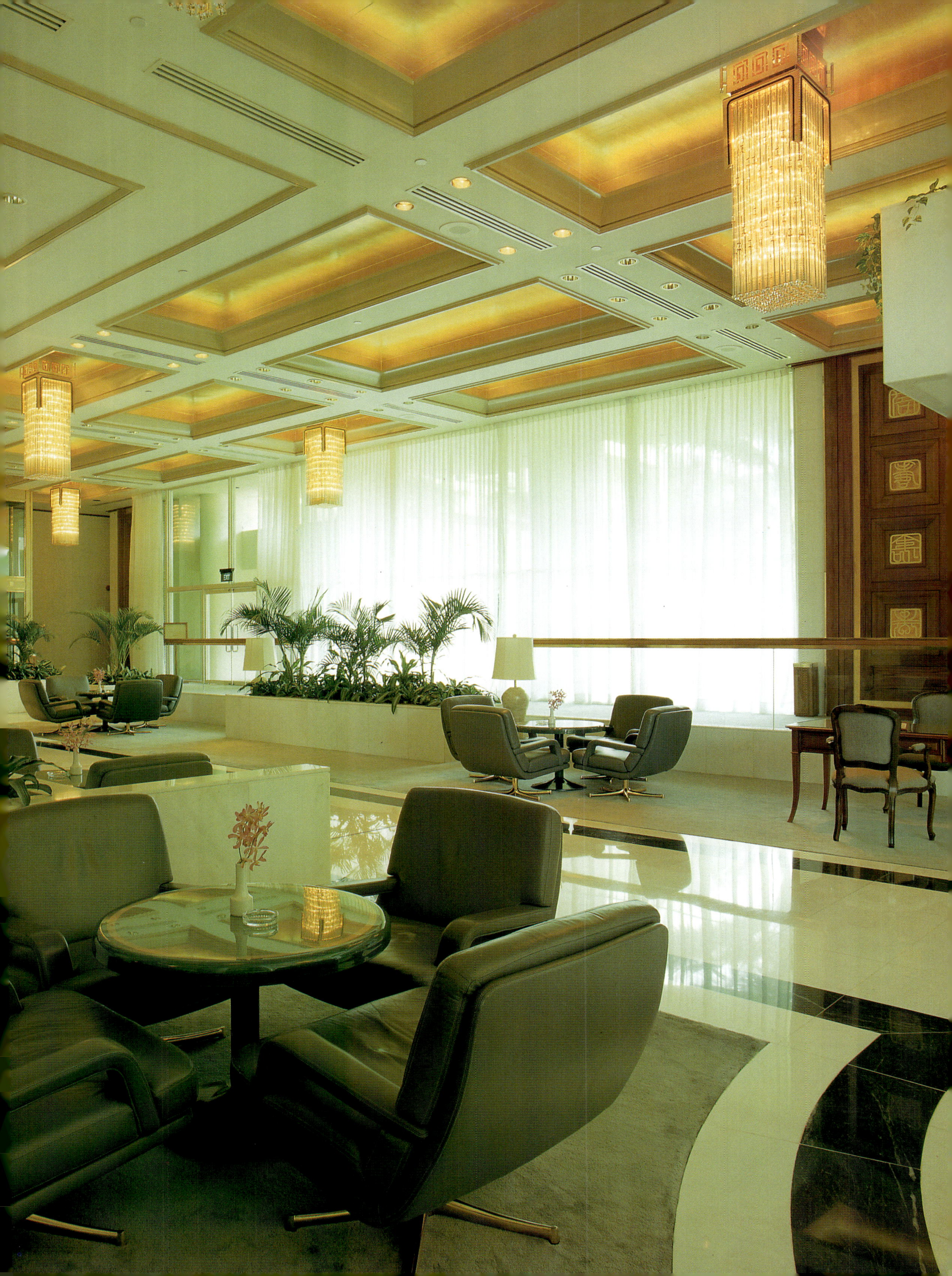

5

6   7

58——Shangri-La Hotel Singapore

8
9

5:「ヴァリー・ウイング」の地下にあるシンガポールのホテルで最大規模の「ヘルス・クラブ」の屋内プール。他にジム、サウナなどがある。6, 7: 日本料理レストラン「なだ万」。寿司カウンター、レストラン・エリア、畳の間がある。8: コンチネンタル料理のレストラン「ラトゥール」。組格子の天井、オーストリア製のクリスタル・シャンデリアで飾られ、クリストフルの銀製品が使われている。9: 幅広い中華料理を提供する「シャン・パレス」。ランチ・タイムの"飲茶"は100品目が用意され、シンガポールでも一級のレストランと評価が高い。その他の飲食施設として、「コーヒー・ガーデン」、「ウォーターフォール・カフェ」、「ロビー・ラウンジ」、「ザナデュー・ディスコ」、「ピーコック・バー」がメイン・ビルディングを中心に置かれている。

5: In the basement of the Valley Wing is the largest *Health Club* of any Singapore hotel, with an indoor pool, gym and sauna. 6, 7: *Nadaman* Japanese restaurant has a sushi counter, dining area and private tatami rooms. 8: *Latour* restaurant serves Continental cuisine and features a latticework ceiling, Austrian crystal chandeliers and Christofle silverware. 9: *Shang Palace* serves a wide range of Chinese cuisine, including 100 different *dim sum* dishes at lunchtime, and has earned a reputation as one of Singapore's finest Chinese restaurants. Other eating and drinking facilities, located mostly in the Main Building, include the *Coffee Garden, Waterfall Café, Lobby Lounge, Xanadu Disco* and *Peacock Bar*.

Great Hotels of the World: vol. 4 — 59

10-16: 最上階につくられた最高級の部屋「マラッカ・スイート(約250㎡)」。応接間、会議室、主寝室、浴室、キッチン、独立した客寝室(浴室つき)から構成される。また、「ヴァリー・ウイング」に置かれたスタンダードの112室は「デラックス・ルーム」と呼ばれ、52㎡もの面積がある。なお、「メイン・ビルディング」と「ヴァリー・ウイング」を結ぶ通路にセキュリティが常駐し、ウイング宿泊者以外は入館できない。

10-16: The deluxe *Malacca Suite* is situated on the top floor of the Valley Wing and has an area totalling some 250 square meters (2,700 sq. ft.). It includes a drawing room, meeting room, master bedroom, bathroom, kitchen, and independent guest bedroom (with bath). Each of the Valley Wing's 112 standard *Deluxe Rooms* is 52 square meters (560 sq. ft.) in area. Security personnel are stationed along the paths connecting the Valley Wing with the Tower Wing, and only guests staying in the Valley Wing are allowed to enter.

60 —— Shangri-La Hotel Singapore

15
16

Hotel Inter·Continental Sydney
117 Macquarie Street, Sydney, N, S, W, Australia

オーストラリア発祥の地といわれるシドニーのサーキュラー・キー（1788年、植民地建設のためにイギリス第一艦隊が上陸したところ）に開発されたユニークなホテル。1849年に建てられた旧大蔵省のクラシカルな建物が利用され、その歴史的な建造物を全面的に修復して、その裏手に31階建ての高層宿泊棟を付設した。開業は1935年9月。建築家はシドニーのカン・フィンチ・アンド・パートナーズ、修復コンサルタントはクライヴ・ルーカス・アンド・パートナーズ。

旧大蔵省の中庭はラウンジに改装され、ここに英国植民地時代の意匠を復活した宴会施設と飲食施設が置かれている。さらに高層宿泊棟最上部には、シドニー湾を一望するレストランがつくられた。このホテルは、歴史的建造物を現代に蘇生させた都市開発の好例とみなされている。

Circular Quay in Sydney is an important landmark in Australian history—this was the landing spot, in 1788, of the first fleet of British ships sent to establish a colony. It is also the site of the former Treasury building, constructed in 1849. The historic building was completely restored and remodeled for use as a hotel, and a 31-story guest room tower was constructed in the rear. The resulting structure, the Hotel Inter·Continental Sydney, opened to the public in September 1985.

Architectural design was by the Sydney firm of Kann Finch and Partners, with restoration consultation provided by Clive Lucas and Partners. The former Treasury courtyard was remodeled as a lounge, and there and in the banquet and dining aras one can see evidence of the revival of English colonial-era design. The restaurants atop the high-rise guest wing offer a sweeping view of Sydney Harbour. The hotel is an excellent example of an urban renewal project giving new life and a new purpose to a fine old historic building.

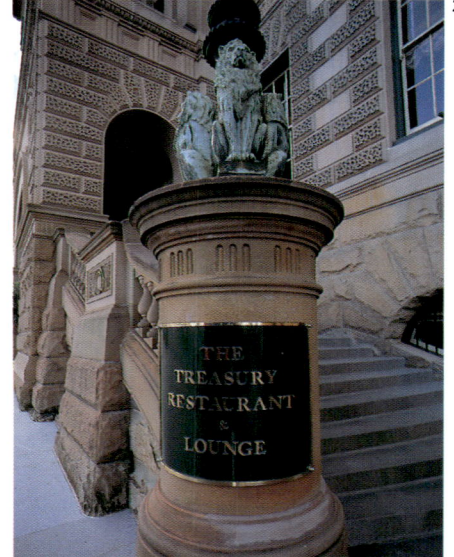

1,2: 旧大蔵省の建物と高層ビルから成るホテル全景。かつての大蔵省入口は外来者用のレストラン入口として利用。3: ホテルの「メイン・エントランス」のドアー表示。4,7,8:「ザ・コルティーレ」と名づけられたラウンジ。旧大蔵省時代には中庭だった。アフタヌーン・ティー、カクテルなどが提供され、夕方にはクラシック音楽の生演奏が楽しめる。1〜2階に飲食施設、3階に宴会施設がある。

1, 2: An overview of the Old Treasury building and the new guest room tower that make up the hotel. The former Treasury entrance is now used as a restaurant entrance for outside visitors. 3: The main entrance door sign. 4, 7, 8: *The Cortile* was once the courtyard of the Old Treasury; it is now a lounge where guests can enjoy afternoon tea, cocktails, and evening performances of classical music. Bars and restaurants are on the first and second floors, with banquet facilities on the third floor.

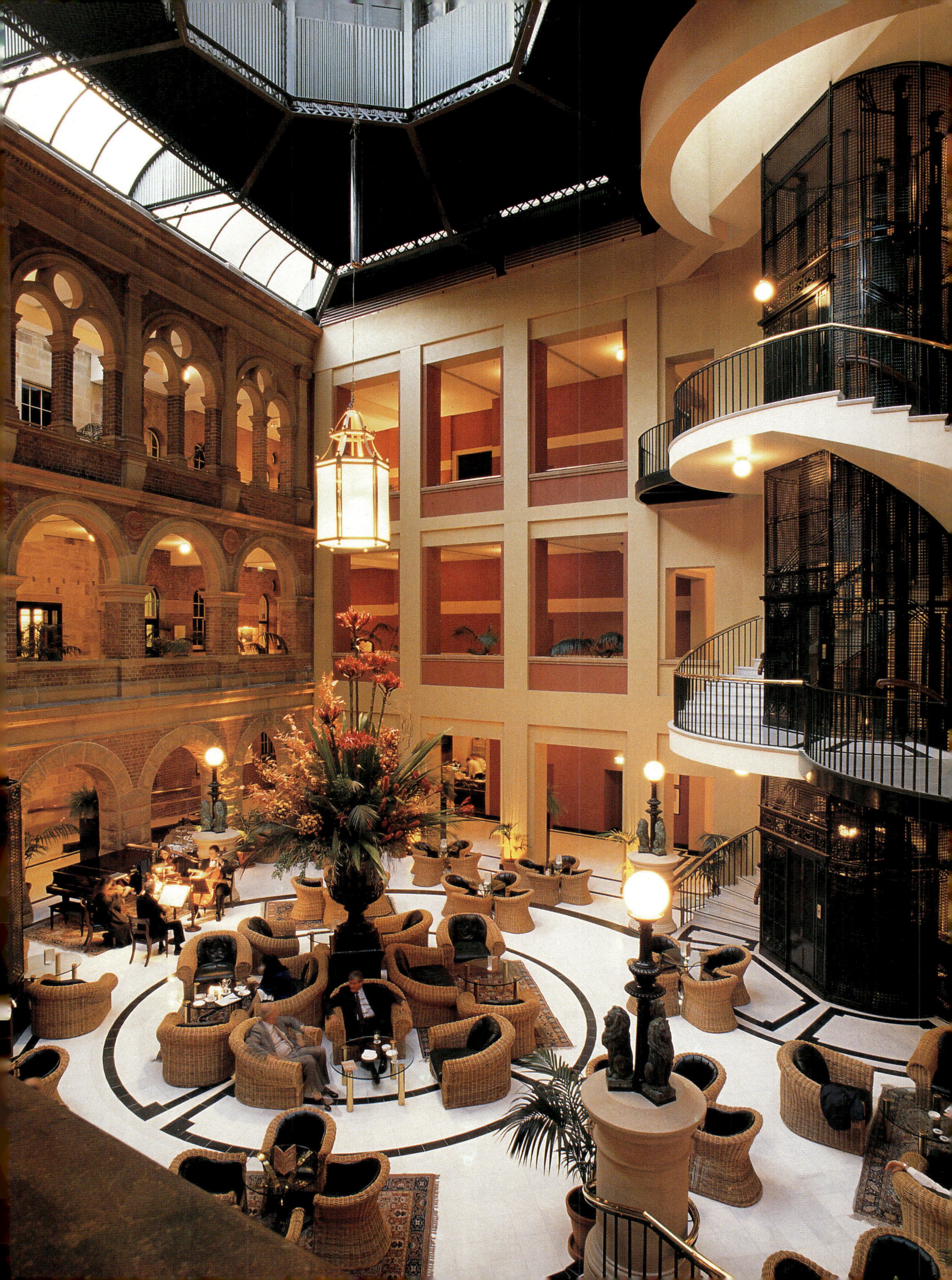

5
6
7
8
9
10

64 —— Hotel Inter · Continental Sydney

11

5: 円形の「エントランス・ホール」。6:「ザ・プリミアーズ・ルーム」は19世紀の州政府要人が会合した部屋。宴会場として使われる。10: 禁煙席を別部屋としたコーヒー・ショップ「カフェ・オペラ」。9, 11–13: 砂岩で建てられた旧大蔵省の建物は修復され、1〜3階のコリドールが残された。中庭には屋根がかけられ、エレガントなお茶を楽しむシドニーの新名所「コルティーレ」に再生された。

5: The circular *Entrance Hall*. 6: *The Premier's Room* was used for meetings of government officials in the 19th century; it is now a banquet room. 10: The *Cafe Opera* has a separate no-smoking room. 9, 11–13: The original corridors on the first three floors of the Old Treasury were preserved when the sandstone-covered building was restored. A roof was added to the original courtyard, and the space was transformed into *The Cortile*, a popular spot to enjoy an elegant tea break and already a Sydney landmark.

12

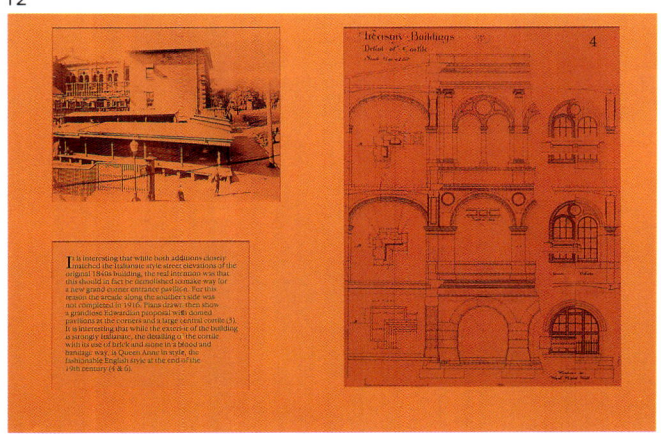

13

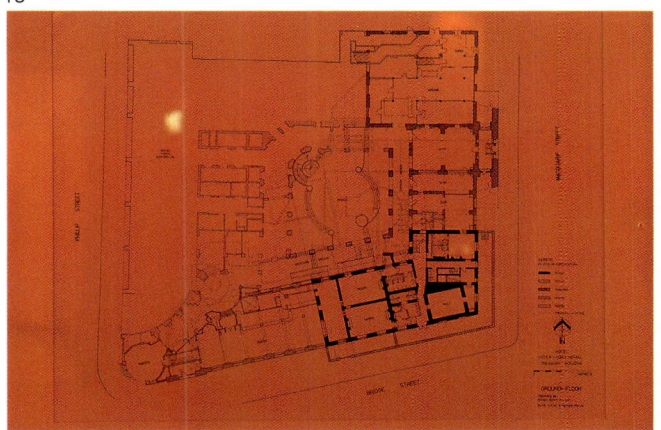

Great Hotels of the World: vol. 4 —— 65

14,15: 2階につくられたメイン・ダイニング「ザ・トレジャリー・レストラン」。その名もずばり大蔵省(トレジャリー)と命名され、同名の「ラウンジ」も付帯する。16: 英国風のパブを模した「ザ・タヴァーン・バー」。アルコール類と食事が楽しめる。17: 宿泊棟最上階(31階)には、シドニー湾、オペラ・ハウスを一望するカクテル・ラウンジ「ザ・トップ・オブ・ザ・トレジャリー」が置かれている。朝食もここで提供される。18: 31階の「ヘルス・クラブ」には、ジム、サウナ、ジャクージなどのフィットネス施設が完備。屋内プールもある。

14, 15: The main dining room, *The Treasury Restaurant*, and *The Treasury Lounge* are on the second floor. **16:** *The Tavern Bar* is an imitation English-style pub, and serves food as well as drinks. **17:** *The Top of the Treasury* cocktail lounge on the top floor offers panoramic views of Sydney Harbour and the Opera House; it also serves breakfast. **18:** The 31st-floor *Health Club* is equipped with a gym, sauna, jacuzzi and other facilities as well as an indoor pool.

66 —— Hotel Inter-Continental Sydney

16
17
18

Great Hotels of the World: vol. 4 — 67

19

20 21

68 —— Hotel Inter · Continental Sydney

22
23

19-23: 5つある最高級の部屋のひとつ「ロイヤル・スイート」(30階)。シッティング・スペースと読書スペースを持つ応接間、会議室、寝室、浴室、で構成される。29〜30階は「エグゼクティブ・フロア」と呼ばれ、29階には特別のサービスを行なう「エグゼクティブ・エクストラ・クラブ」があり、朝食、カクテル、お茶などはここで提供され、料金は宿泊料金に含まれる。

19-23: The 30th-floor *Royal Suite* is one of five top-class suites. The main drawing room includes a "sitting area" and a "reading area"; there is also a meeting room, bedroom and bathroom. The 29th and 30th floors are the hotel's "Executive Floors." Guests staying on the 29th floor also receive special *Executive Extra Club* service, including breakfast, cocktail and tea service, included in the price of their rooms.

Great Hotels of the World: vol. 4 — 69

The Dubai International Hotel
P.O. Box 10001, Dubai, United Arab Emirates

　産油国アラブ首長国連邦の港湾都市ドバイに建てられたホテル、ザ・ドバイ・インターナショナルの開業は1979年。15万m²の広大な敷地に、わずか400室の低層ホテルが建設された。

　1970年代後期は、あり余るオイル・ダラーが中東の都市に大型ホテルを次々に開業させた時代であった。アラブのホテルに相応しく、パティオ（中庭）に噴水を置き、それを低層の宿泊棟が囲む。さらにもうひとつのパティオには、砂漠のオアシスをイメージした屋外プールがつくられている。アラブ首長国連邦では、飲酒は御法度。ただし、国際的なホテルのなかだけは治外法権で、このホテルのバーやディスコではアルコール飲料を十分楽しむことができる。フランス料理のレストランは、天井に天幕風照明を取り入れた独特な内装。中国料理レストランも加えられ、国際色も豊かな近代ホテルである。ドバイ・インターナショナルは、ドバイ国際空港からわずか5分の位置にある便利な空港ホテルとしても知られている。

●●●

　The Dubai International Hotel opened in 1979 in the Gulf port city of Dubai in the oil-producing United Arab Emirates.

　The late 1970's was an era that saw abundant oil money financing massive construction of large-scale hotels throughout the Mideast; however, this low-rise facility, stretching over a 150,000 square meter (37 acre) site, has a mere 400 guest rooms. Appropriately for its location, the hotel features a fountained patio. An outdoor pool with a desert oasis motif occupies another patio.

　Although alcohol is forbidden in the country, an exception to the law is made for international hotels, and guests may order alcoholic beverages at the bars and disco here. The French restaurant has an unusual interior featuring cloth-covered ceiling lighting, and there is also a Chinese restaurant, giving the hotel a modern, international outlook. And, with a location just five minutes from the international airport, The Dubai International also serves as a convenient airport hotel.

1, 2: 砂漠の都市ドバイの国際空港ホテルとしても機能する施設。写真2、5の右上にドバイ国際空港が見える。建築家はアレンコ・アーキテクチュラル・アンド・エンジニアリング・コンサルタンツのA・A・アル・ムーサ。2年の工期で完成した。3: ホテル・スタッフの大部分が外国人。4, 5, 11: 中庭の「ミラージュ・プール」。同名の「バー」も付設。夜は"バーベキュー・ナイト"と名づけられた実演つきのディナーが楽しめる。

●●●

1, 2: The Dubai International Hotel serves the desert city of Dubai as well as nearby Dubai International Airport. (The airport is visible in the upper right-hand portion of photos no. 2 and no. 5). The architectural design was the work of A.A. Al Moosa of Arenco Architectural & Engineering Consultants, and construction was completed over a period of two years. 3: Most of the hotel staff are non-natives. 4, 5, 11: *Le Mirage Pool* and *Le Mirage Bar* are located in the courtyard. Evening diners can enjoy a "Barbecue Night" performance here.

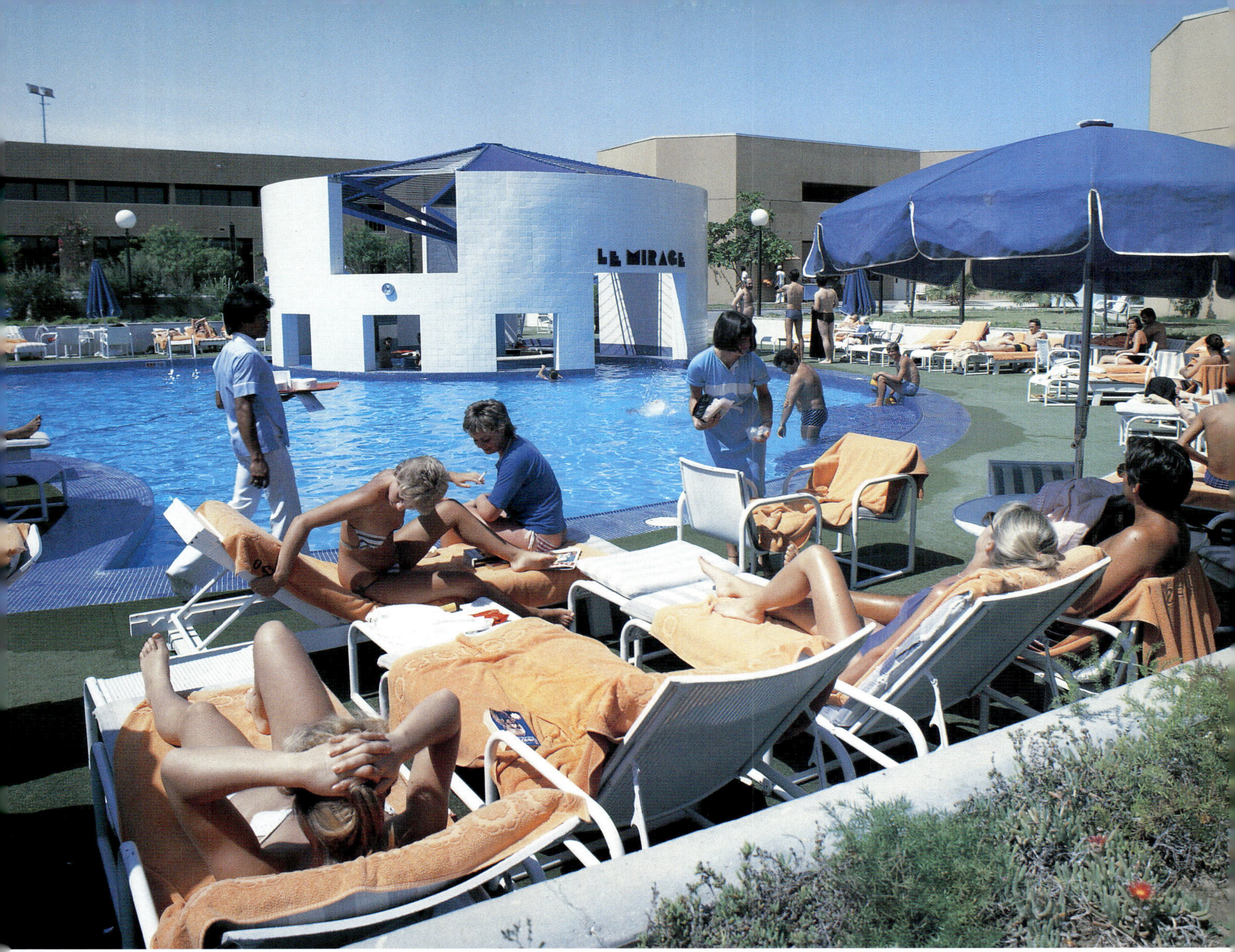
LE MIRAGE

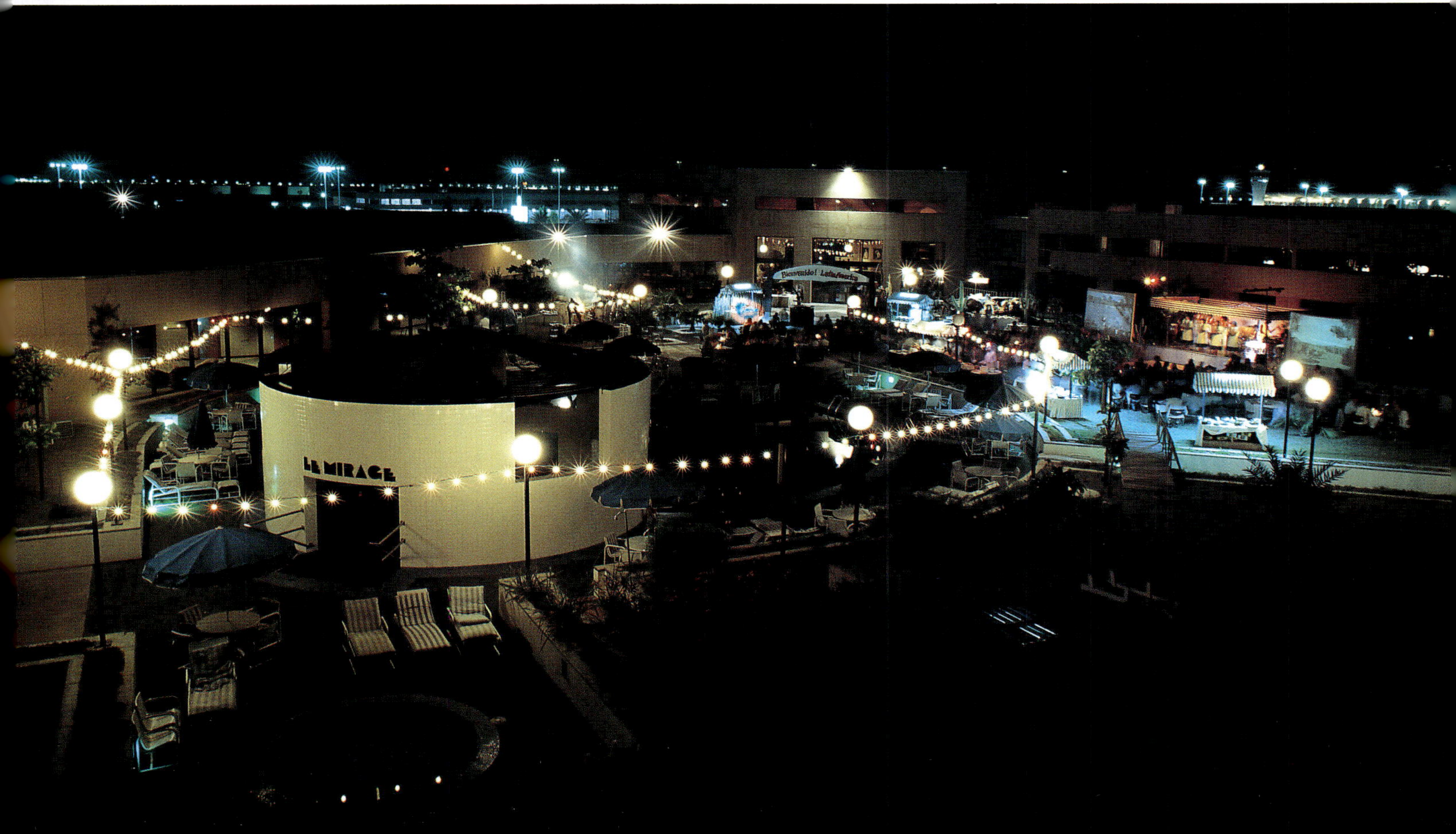
LE MIRAGE

6
7
8
9
10
11

72——The Dubai International Hotel

12

6：大宴会場「ザ・ファルコン・ホール」。7,8：〝その実を食べれば浮世の苦しみを忘れる〟といわれるロートス(夢楽樹)の林をイメージした「ロビー」。9：コーヒーショップ「ザ・ブラスリー」。10：ディスコ「スタジオ・セヴン」。12,13：天井を布地照明カバーで飾ったメイン・ダイニング「カフェ・ロワイヤル」はショーが楽しめるフランス料理レストラン。他に中華レストランも設けられている。14：噴水のある中庭「パティオ」。

6: *The Falcon Hall* is a large banquet area. 7, 8: According to Greek legend, eating the fruit of the lotus lets one forget the cares of the world. The *Lobby* creates the image of a lotus forest. 9: *The Brasserie* coffee shop. 10: *Studio 7* disco. 12, 13: The design of *Cafe Royal*, the main dining room, incorporates unusual cloth-covered ceiling lighting. French cuisine is the specialty, and there is also a show. The hotel also has a Chinese restaurant. 14: The *Patio* courtyard is equipped with fountains.

13

14

Great Hotels of the World: vol.4 —— 73

15, 16: 2層にわたる最高級の部屋「シェイク・スィート」。ドバイの統治者でもあり、アラブ首長国の副大統領でもあるホテルのオーナーにちなんで名づけられた。1階に応接間、会議室、キッチン、小寝室、2階に主寝室、浴室、休息スペースがある。
17: 応接間と寝室から成る「グラナダ・スイート」。
18: 2つのベッドを備えたスタンダードの部屋「ツイン・ルーム」。

●●●

15, 16: The top-class *Sheikh Suite* spans two floors. It is named after the hotel owner, who is also the Ruler of Dubai and Vice President of the United Arab Emirates. A drawing room, meeting room, kitchen and small bedroom are on the first floor, and a master bedroom, bathroom and rest area are on the second floor. **17**: A drawing room and separate bedroom make up the *Granada Suite*. **18**: A standard *Twin Room* with two beds.

74——The Dubai International Hotel

17

18

Great Hotels of the World: vol. 4 ——— 75

Athens Ledra Marriott Hotel
115 Syngrou Avenue, Athens 117 45, Greece

　ギリシァの首都アテネは地中に埋もれた遺跡のおびただしさから、新しいホテルの開発がきわめて難しい都市として知られている。そのパルテノン神殿が立つアクロポリスを望む市街地に、1983年、アテン・レドラ・マリオット・ホテルが開業した。米国のホテル企業、マリオット・ホテルズ・アンド・リゾーツが運営する9階建、258室の近代ホテルである。

　アクロポリスからピレウス港（エーゲ海クルーズの出航地）まで見わたせる屋上にバーと大プールが設けられ、アテネ市全域を一望する絶好のナイト・スポットとして人気が高い。また地下には、ギリシァでは珍しいポリネシア・レストランがつくられ、広東料理や鉄板焼コーナーまである。アメリカン・タッチのフレンドリーなサービスが好評の人気ホテルである。

●●●

　The Greek capital of Athens, with its numerous buried ruins, is said to be a difficult place to build a new hotel. Despite this, though, in 1983 the Athens Ledra Marriott Hotel was erected in a section of the city overlooking the Acropolis, site of the Parthenon. The nine-story, 258-room hotel is managed by the American hotel company Marriott Hotels and Resorts.

　The large rooftop pool offers bathers a spectacular view stretching from the Acropolis to the port of Piraeus, where cruise ships sailing the Aegean start their journeys. The rooftop bar, with its view of the entire city of Athens, has become a popular nightspot. On the basement level is one of Greece's few Polynesian restaurants; it also serves Cantonese food and Japanese *teppanyaki* dishes. The hotel has become popular for its friendly, American-style service.

1,2: アテネ市の中心部から車で10分、ピレウス港やエリニコン国際空港から30分の市街地にある。4: アクロポリス、リカベトスの丘など、アテネ全域を見渡せるホテル屋上のプール。「パノラマ・バー」があり、夏には同名の「レストラン」も開店する。3,5: 入口を入った左側に位置する「レセプション」。右側にロビー・バー「クリスタル・ラウンジ」がある。

●●●

1, 2: The hotel is located within the city, ten minutes by car from downtown Athens and 30 minutes from the port of Piraeus and Ellinikon International Airport. 4: The rooftop pool provides a stunning view of the Acropolis, Lycabettus hill and all of Athens. Also on the roof are the *Panorama Bar* and, open only in the summertime, the *Panorama Restaurant*. 3, 5: The *Reception Desk* is located to the left of entrance, and the *Crystal Lounge* lobby bar to the right.

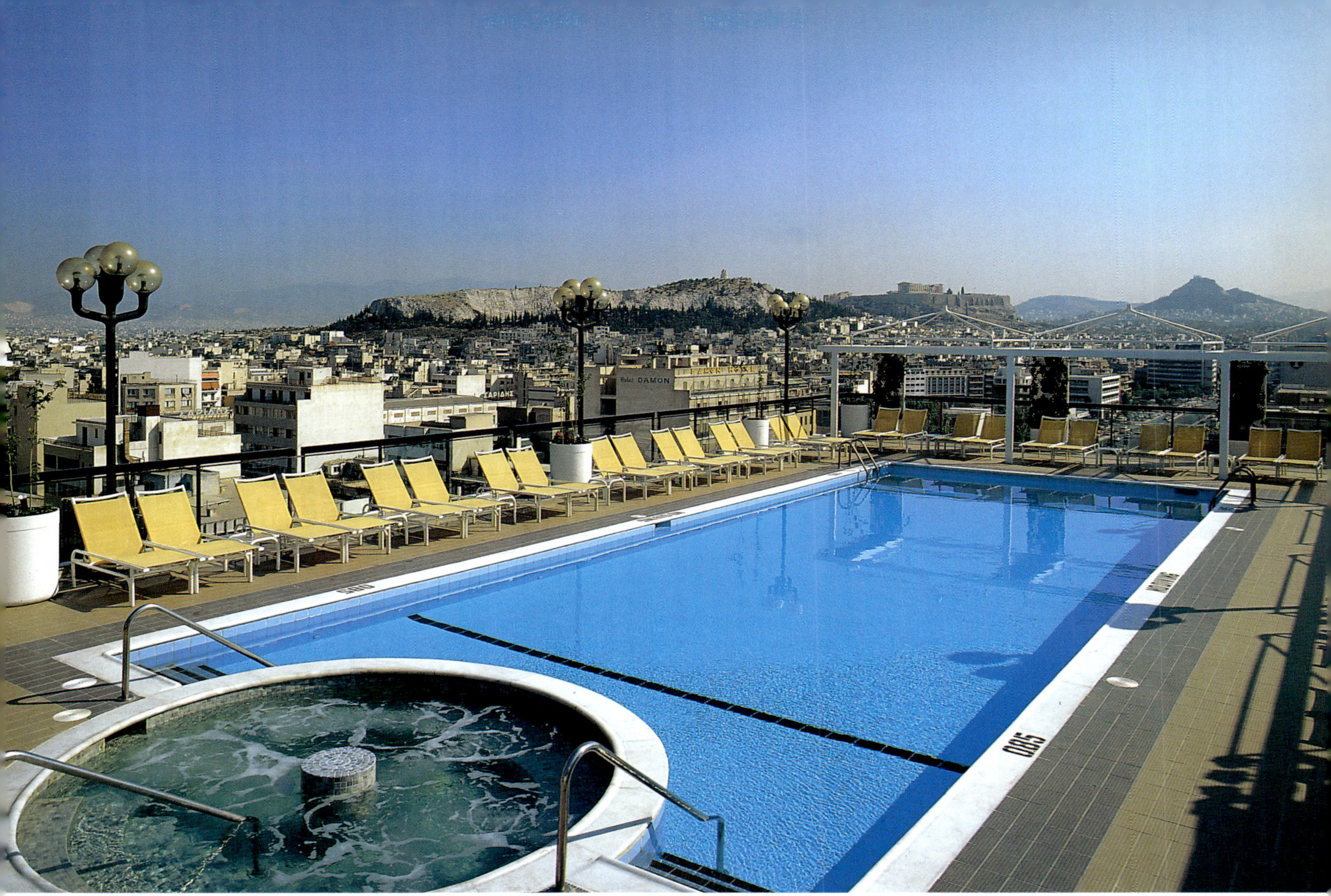

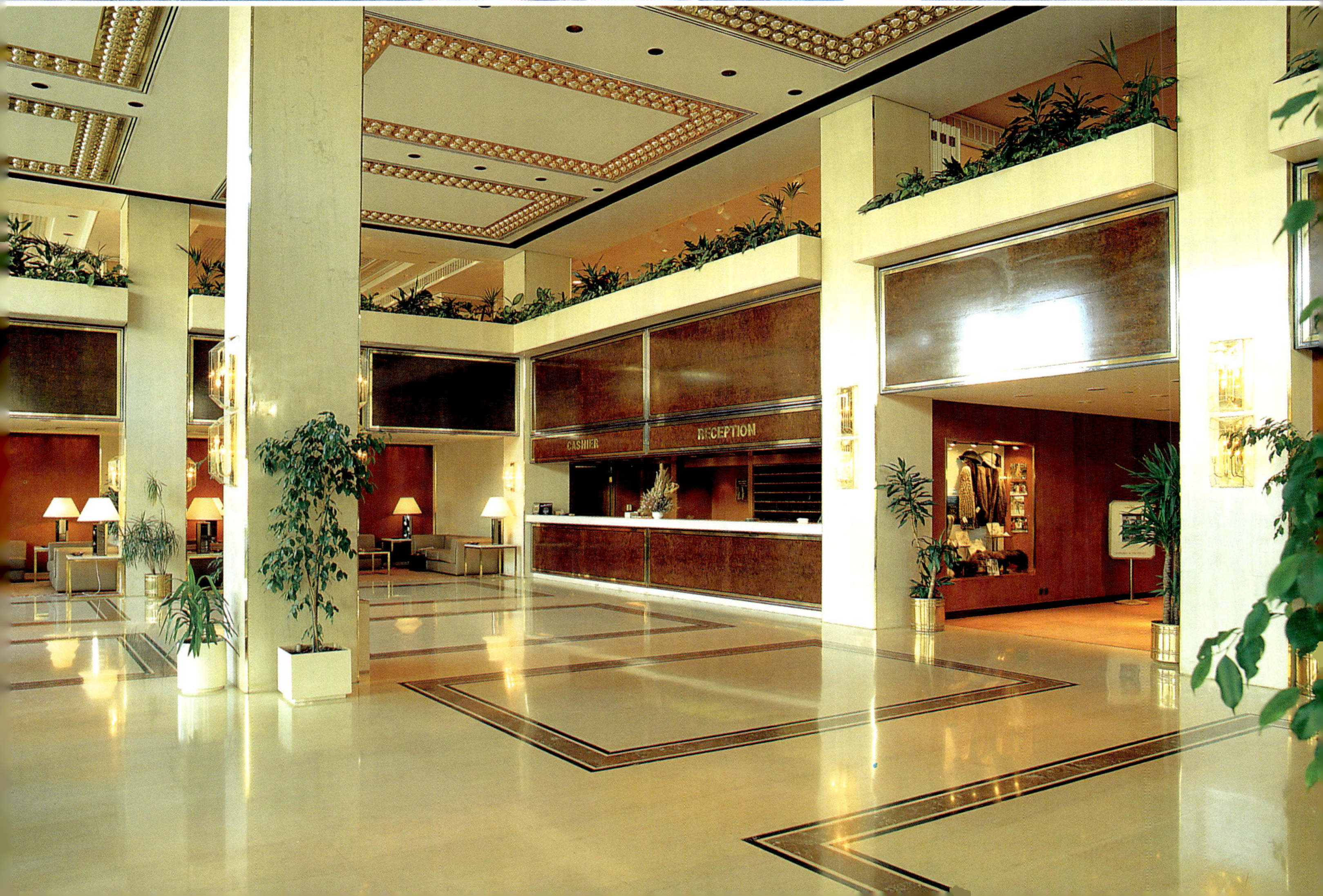
CASHIER
RECEPTION

6: グルメ・レストラン「ザ・レドラ・グリル」。アメリカ牛から魚貝類まで幅広い料理を提供する。7,8: 地下につくられた「コナ・カイ・レストラン」。ポリネシア料理、中華料理から鉄板焼まで楽しめる。9: ギリシァ料理、コンチネンタル料理、ビュッフェが選べるレストラン「ゼフィロス（西風）」。10: スタンダードの部屋「ツイン・ルーム」。

6: *The Ledra Grill* offers a varied gourmet menu ranging from American beef to seafood. 7, 8: The underground *Kona Kai Restaurant* serves Polynesian and Chinese cuisine and also has a Japanese *teppanyaki* grill. 9: The buffet at *Zephyros Restaurant* offers a choice of Greek and Continental dishes. 10: A standard *Twin Room*.

78——Athens Ledra Marriott Hotel

9
10

Great Hotels of the World: vol.4 —— 79

11

11-15: 会議スペースを持つ応接間、寝室、浴室から成る「プレジデンシャル・スイート」。白とブルーでコーディネイトした近代的な部屋。

11–15: The modern *Presidential Suite* is coordinated in white and blue, and includes a drawing room with meeting area, bedroom and bathroom.

12 13

Athens Ledra Marriott Hotel

14
15

Hotel La Mamounia
Avenue Bab Jdid, Marrakech, Morocco

　北アフリカのアトラス山脈を借景とした古都マラケシュのホテルである。18世紀のスルタン、モハメッド・ベン・アブドラーは、第一王子ムーレイ・マムーンに結婚式のプレゼントとして大庭園を贈った。81,000m²に及ぶ庭園と離宮は当時"エル・マムーン"と呼ばれ、王子はそこを休息の場としてしばしば足を運んだという。1923年、この庭園を利用して3階建、100室のホテルが建てられ、王子の名を取って「ホテル・ラ・マムーニャ」と命名された。オーナーはモロッコ国営鉄道会社、建築家はA・マルキージオとアンリ・プロスト。伝統的なムーア・アラブ様式とアール・デコ様式を融合させ、独特の内装を取り入れた。

　1953年、近代設備を導入する増改築が行なわれ、5階建、200室のホテルが完成。1977年には、内部の修復が行なわれた。開業以来、モロッコ随一の欧米の要人が滞在するホテルとして知られている。

Hotel La Mamounia is located in the old capital city of Marrakech, overlooking the Atlas Mountains. Its history began in the 18th century, when Sultan Mohamed ben Abdollah presented an enormous garden to his eldest son, Prince Moulay Mamoun, as a wedding gift. The 81,000 square meter (20 acre) garden and the royal villa built within were known at the time as "El Mamoun," and were often visited by the prince.

In 1923 a three-story, 100-room hotel was constructed within the garden and was named after the prince. The original owner was the Moroccan National Railroad Company. The architects, A. Marchisio and Henri Prost, combined traditional Moorish-Arab design with Art Deco style elements to create an unusual interior. In 1953 the hotel was remodeled and modern facilities were added; at the same time it was enlarged to five stories and 200 rooms. In 1977 the interior was again renovated. Since its opening, the hotel has been famous as a stopping place for important visitors from Europe and America.

1,2：高い外壁をめぐらしたホテルの最上階から見た「プール」と「大庭園」。雪をいただくアトラス山脈が見える。3：入口に待機するポーター。4：入口の「レセプション」後方に位置する「ホール」。大シャンデリアとヒマラヤ杉の装飾天井は開業時からのオリジナル。

1, 2: View of the pool and large garden as seen from the top floor. The snow-peaked Atlas Mountains are also visible. The hotel is surrounded by high outer walls. 3: A porter stationed at the entrance. 4: The *Hall*, behind the entrance *Reception* area, retains its original large chandeliers and Himalayan cedar ceiling ornaments.

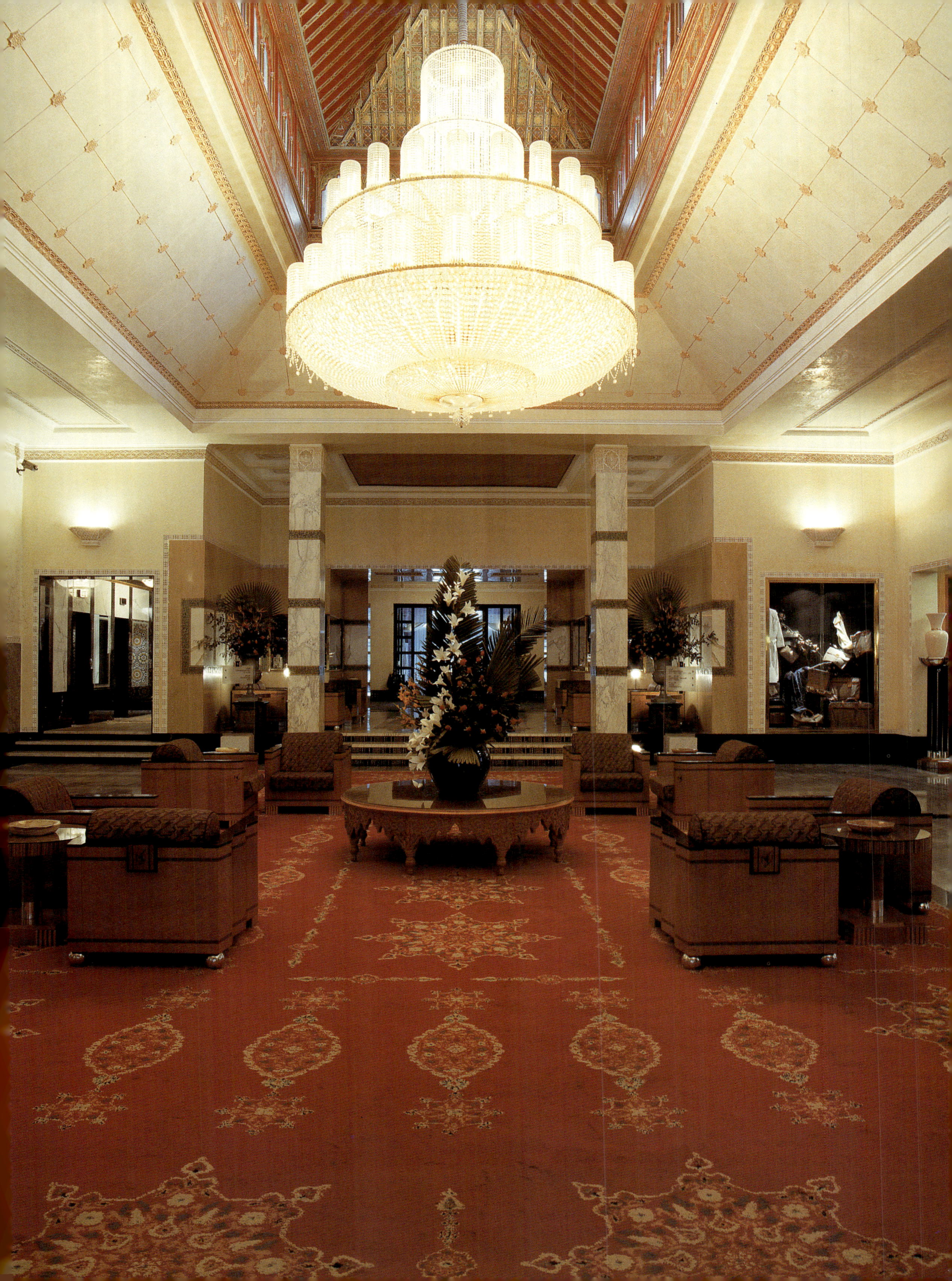

5:「ホール」から続くコロネードの左右に配された「ロビー」。至るところにアール・デコのデザインが取り入れられている。使われている椅子は、1929年にジュール・ルルーが製作した有名な"ルルー・アームチェア"のレプリカ。他にアール・デコのデザイナーだったジャック・ルールマンのデザインも取り入れられている。6,7: ヒマラヤ杉の寄せ木細工でデザインされた「コンシェルジュ・デスク」と「チェック・イン・デスク」。8-10: 開業時の「ロビー」だった現在の「ゲスト・ホール」。アンダルシア風の池が付設されている。中2階部分をアール・デコ様式でコーディネイト。開業時は、階段が部屋に通じる唯一のルートだった。

5: Continuing past the *Hall* is the colonnaded *Lobby*. Art Deco design is prominent throughout the hotel. The chairs here are replicas of 1929 Leleu armchairs crafted by designer Jules Leleu. The work of Art Deco designer Jacques Ruhlmann can also be seen. 6, 7: The *Concierge Desk* and *Check-in Desk* use Himalayan cedar marquetry panels. 8–10: The original

84 —— Hotel La Mamounia

8

lobby is now used as a *Guest Hall*, and includes an Andalusian-style pond. The mezzanine is decorated in Art Deco style. The staircase was originally the only route to the guest rooms.

9

10

Great Hotels of the World: vol. 4 — 85

11, 12: 無蓋の四輪馬車（カレーシュ）が3台置かれたレストラン「ラ・カレーシュ」。テラス部分は朝食ビュッフェに使われる。13: プールサイドのレストラン「レ・トロワ・パルミエ（3本のヤシ）」。プールに3本のヤシの樹が立つ。14, 15: 6個所あるレストランのうちのメイン・ダイニング「マラケシュ・ランペリアル」。マラケシュの町を描いた18枚の油絵が壁を飾っている。ミシュラン3ツ星の高名レストラン、パリの「リュカ・キャルトン」のシェフ、アラン・サンデランスの料理を受け継ぐレストラン。インテリアは20世紀初頭の豪華客船内部を模している。昼食にはビュッフェも楽しめる。

●●●

11, 12: Three antique carriages are found inside *La Caleche* ("The Carriage") restaurant. Breakfast is served on the terrace. 13: *Les Trois Palmiers*, the poolside restaurant, is named for the three palm trees in the pool area. 14, 15: The *Marrakech L'Imperiale* main dining room is one of six restaurants. Eighteen paintings of the city of Marrakech hang on the walls. The French cuisine is prepared in the tradition of master chef Alain Senderens of the Michelin three-star Parisian restaurant Lucas-Carton. A luncheon buffet is served at midday. The interior is designed to resemble an elegant, early-20th-century passenger ship.

86 —— Hotel La Mamounia

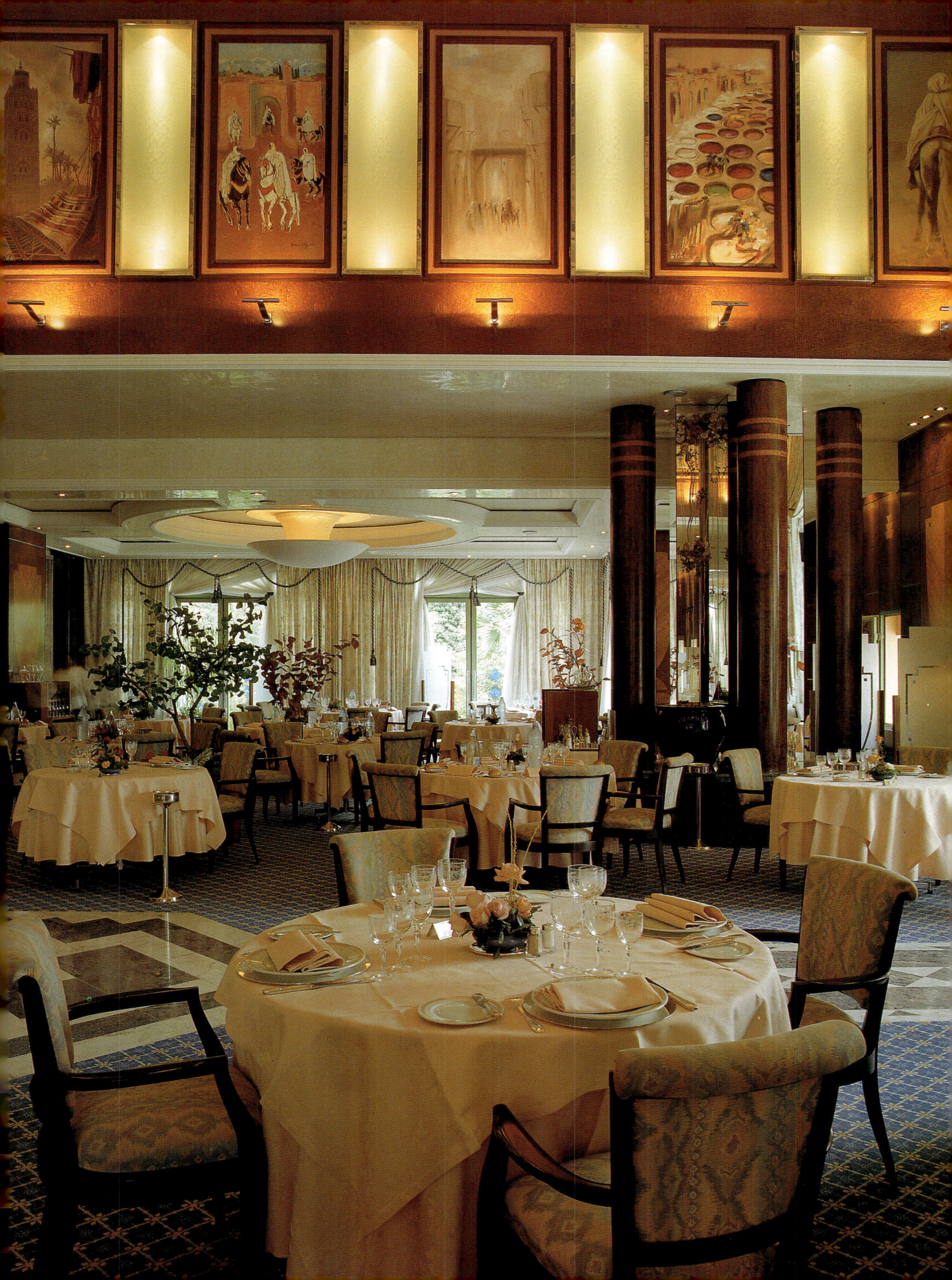

16-18: モロッコ料理専門のレストラン「ル・レストラン・マロカン・ド・ラ・マムーニャ」。19-21: 49セットあるスイート・ルームのひとつ"オリエント・イクスプレス"。ロンドン―イスタンブール間を走った〝オリエント急行〞のデラックス・コンパートメントを再現。応接間、寝室、バー、小キッチンがある。22-24: 伝統的なムーア様式で装飾した部屋「スイート・ゲブス（漆喰装飾の間）」。

16-18: *Le Restaurant Marocain de la Mamounia* specializes in Moroccan cuisine. 19-21: The *Orient Express*, one of 49 suites, is inspired by a deluxe compartment on the luxurious London-to-Istanbul train of the same name. It comprises a drawing room, bedroom, bar and small kitchen. 22-24: Traditional Moorish decor characterizes the *Suite Gebs*.

88 —— Hotel La Mamounia

19

20  21

22

23 24

Great Hotels of the World: vol.4 —— 89

25-32：英国首相だったサー・ウインストン・チャーチル夫妻がしばしば避寒に訪れた部屋が、「スイート・チャーチル」として4階に保存されている。この部屋はもとは3階にあった。チャーチルが愛用した傘や帽子、未完の油絵（アトラス山脈と空想上の湖が描かれている）が残されている。彼はこの部屋に付属した小さなベッドがある「控室」やヴェランダで絵を描くことを好んだという。

25-32: British Prime Minister Winston Churchill and his wife often visited here to escape the winter cold, and the room where they stayed has been preserved as the *Suite Churchill* on the fourth floor, although the suite was originally located on the third floor. Churchill's umbrella and hat are still here, along with an unfinished oil painting of the Atlas Mountains and an imaginary lake. Churchill was said to have enjoyed painting in the small waiting room adjoining the suite as well as on the veranda.

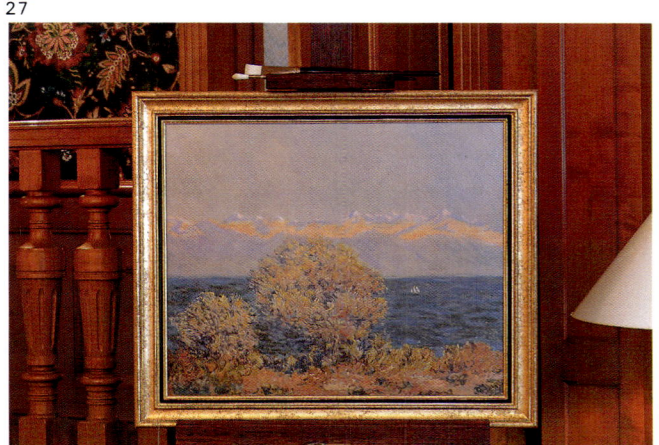

28

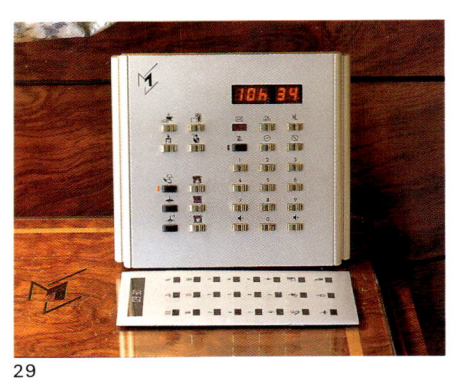

29

30

31

32

Great Hotels of the World: vol. 4 — 91

Hotel Palais Jamai
Bab El Guissa, Fez, Morocco

　世界最大の迷路といわれるモロッコの古都フェズのメディーナ（旧市街）にあるホテル。ジャマイという名が示すように、この建物は、1879年、この地方の領主で、スルタン・ムーレイ・ハッサンとの血縁によって勢力を拡大したジャマイ家の別邸として建てられた。アンダルシア風の庭園を持つムーア様式の代表的なモロッコの大邸宅だった。

　1930年、ホテルとして開業することになり、旧館につながる新館が造られ、旧館のオリジナル装飾である"渦巻漆喰装飾"、"陶タイル装飾""アーチ門"などがみごとに修復された。旧館のスイート・ルームは、むかしハーレムとして使われていたもの。また新館は、旧館の雰囲気を壊さないように内装が施された。パレ・ジャマイはマラケシュのホテル・ラ・マムーニャとともに、モロッコを代表する二大ホテルといわれている。

　This hotel is built in the former market area of the old Moroccan capital city of Fez, an area sometimes called "the world's largest labyrinth." It was named after the Jamai family, relatives of the region's ruling feudal lord, Sultan Moulay-Hassan, and it was built in 1879 as the Jamai family mansion. With its Andalusian-style garden and Moorish-style exterior walls, it is a typical Moroccan mansion of that period.

　In 1930 it opened as a hotel, and a new wing was added, with its design carefully planned to harmonize with the original, older wing. At that time the original decorations, including the scrolled plasterwork, brightly colored glazed tiles and arched gates, were beautifully restored. The "Suite room" in the old wing was formerly used as a harem area. This hotel and Hotel La Mamounia in Marrakech are known as Morocco's two leading hotels.

1：中庭にアンダルシア風の庭園とプールを置いた6階建のホテル。左端の建物が以前ハーレムとして使われていた。2：「メイン・エントランス」のドアの上に取りつけられた装飾庇。3：「コンシェルジュ」。4：ハーレムの部屋だった「アンバサダー・スイート」。陶タイル（ゼリージ）が床と壁の下部に張られ、壁の上部を伝統的な漆喰装飾（ゲブス）が蔽っている。

1: A magnificent Andalusian-style garden and pool are located in the courtyard of this six-story hotel. The building at the upper left was formerly used as a harem. 2: Decorative eaves adorn the upper portion of the main entranceway door. 3: The *Concierge* desk. 4: The *Ambassador Suite*, a former harem room. The floor and the lower part of the walls are covered with "Zelliges" glazed tiles, while the upper portions of the walls are decorated with traditional "Gebs" scrolled plasterwork.

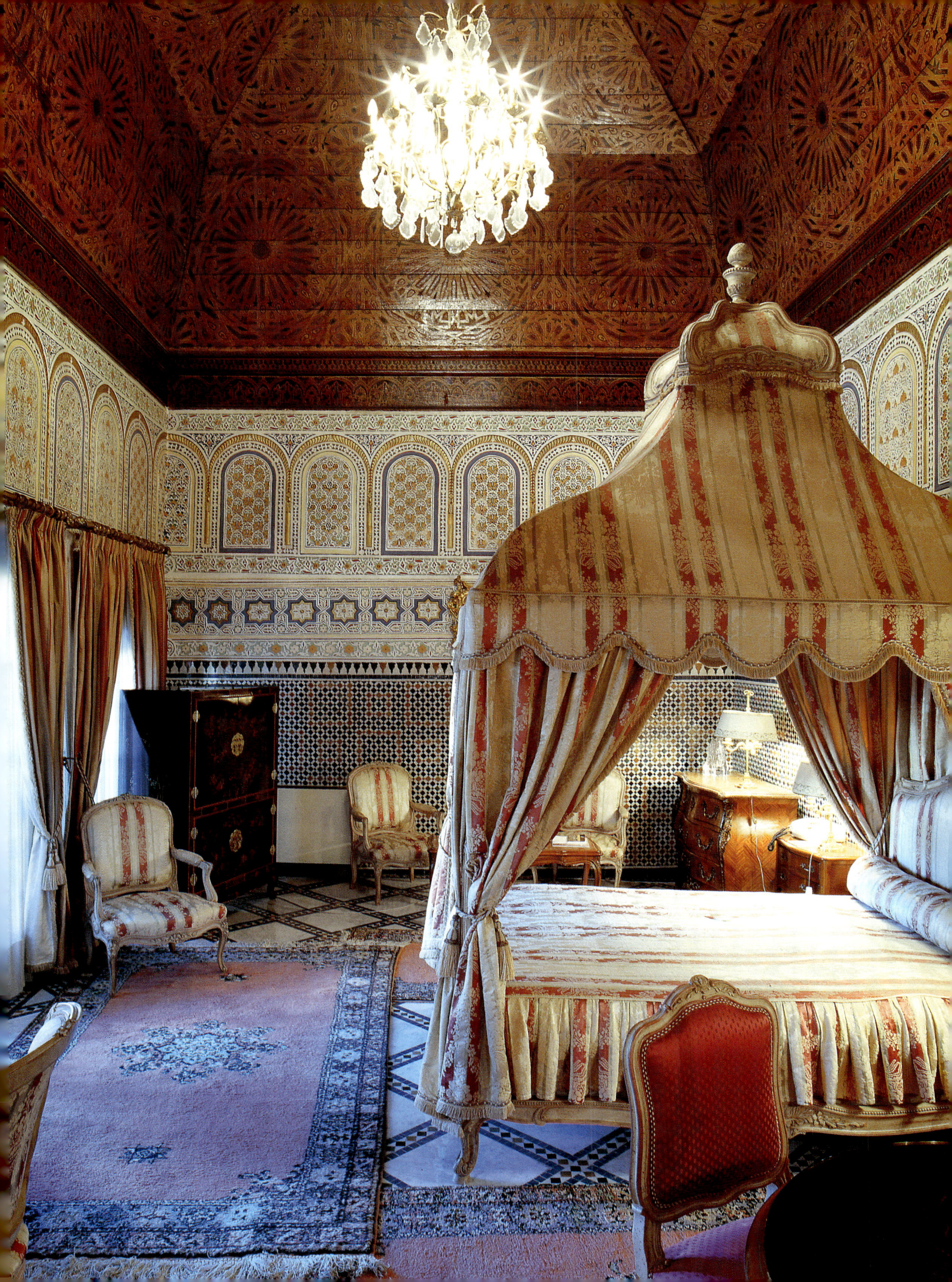

94——Hotel Palais Jamai

7

5, 6: 陶タイル（ゼリージ）で装飾された長い「レセプション・カウンター」が置かれた「ロビー」。「レセプション」の壁を飾る絵はモロッコの宮殿生活を描いたもの。**7-9:** 昼食に使われるレストラン「ラ・ジェニナ」のテラス部分。屋外プールの下段にはアンダルシア様式の庭園がつくられ、噴水や日陰の休息スペースもある。

5, 6: The long *reception counter* in the *lobby* is covered in "Zelliges" glazed tiles. The painting in the reception area depicts life in the Moroccan royal palace. **7–9:** The terrace portion of *La Djenina* restaurant, which serves lunch. At the lower level of the outdoor pool is an Andalusian-style garden, with a fountain and shady rest areas.

8

9

Great Hotels of the World: vol. 4 —— 95

10, 11: テラス部分と屋内で計200人を収容するレストラン「ラ・ジェニナ」。壁を飾る絵画は、古都フェズの最初の宮殿(イドリス朝・9世紀)を描いたもの。12, 13: モロッコの伝統料理、クスクス(小麦粉のツブを蒸し、上から野菜と肉のシチューをかけた料理)、タジン(土鍋のスープ)などを提供するレストラン「アル・フェッシャ」。内部はいくつもの小部屋に区切られ、民族音楽や舞踊も楽しめる。

10, 11: Including its terrace and outdoor areas, *La Djenina* restaurant can accommodate a total of 200 diners. The mural on the wall shows the first royal palace in the ancient capital of Fez, dating back to the Idrus dynasty of the 9th century AD. 12, 13: *Al Fassia* restaurant serves such traditional Moroccan dishes as *couscous* (grainy steamed semolina covered with stewed meat and vegetables) and *tagine* (a soup cooked in an earthenware pot). The interior is divided into numerous small rooms, and folk music and dance are performed.

96 —— Hotel Palais Jamai

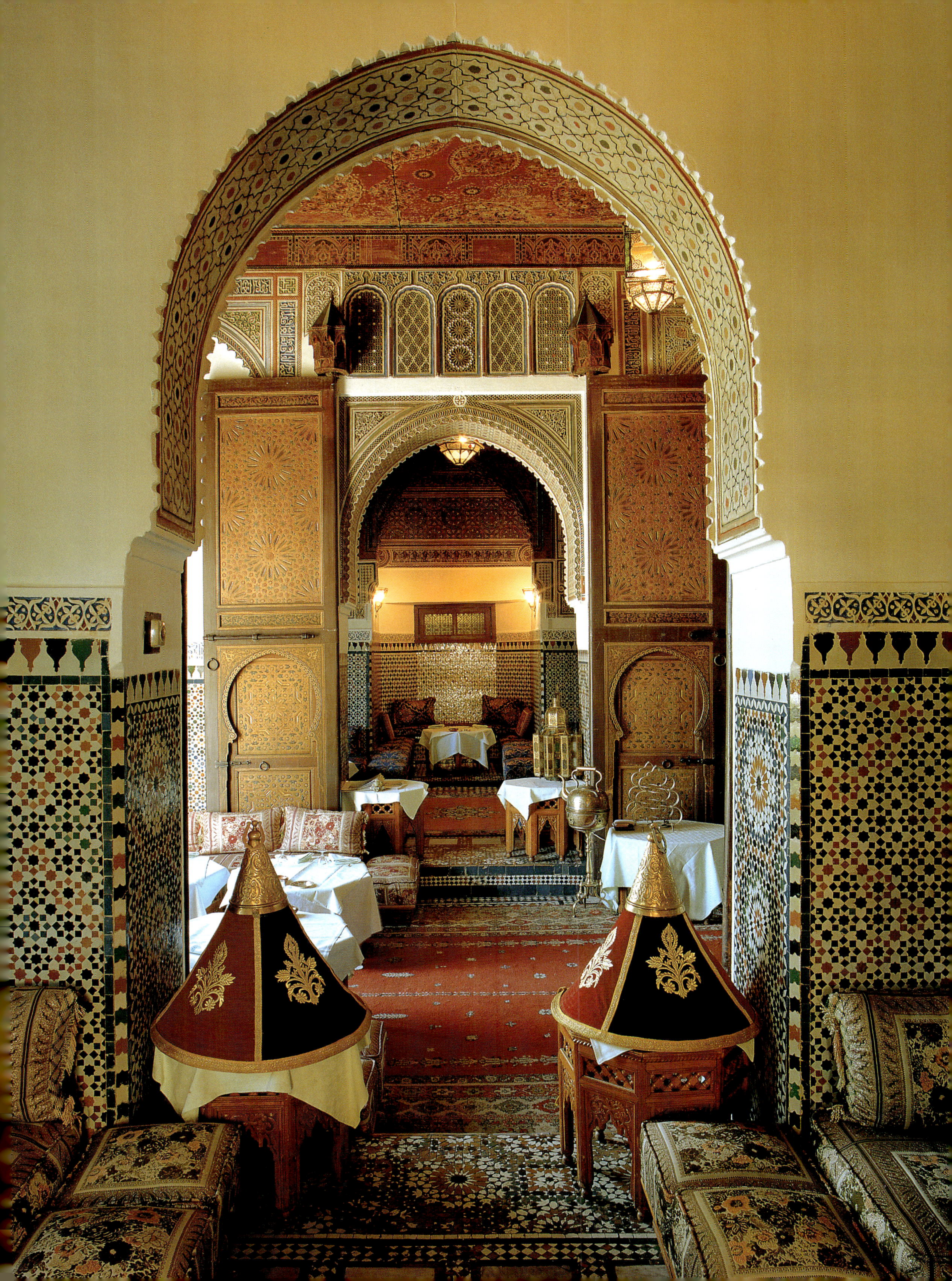

14: モロッコの伝統的装飾で飾られた「リーディング・ルーム」。椅子はルイ14世式。隣りに「コンフェランス・ルーム」がある。15: 屋外プールを見渡すバー「アル・アンダルス」。ほかに「ナイト・クラブ」、"ハマム"と呼ばれる「トルコ風呂」が地下に設けられている。16-21: ハーレムとして使われていた部屋「スイート・ド・ラ・ファヴォリト」。写真16の梁装飾は、木彫りに漆喰を塗った"ムカーナス"と呼ばれるムーア様式独特の内装である。

14: The *Reading Room* features traditional Moroccan decor and Louis XIV—style chairs. Next door is the *Conference Room*. 15: *Al Andalous* bar offers a view of the outdoor pool. The *nightclub* and the "Hammam" turkish baths are located below ground level. 16–21: The *Suite de la Favorite* is a former harem room. The unusual Moorish-style decorative crossbeams in photo no. 16 are "Mouquarnas" plaster-covered wood carvings.

98 —— Hotel Palais Jamai

16

17

18

19

20

21

22

22-26: 10個所あるスイートのひとつ「ル・グラン・ヴィジール」。玄関スペース、応接間、書斎、寝室、浴室、大きなヴェランダで構成され、応接間には手の込んだ木製装飾天井が使われている。27: このスイートのヴェランダから望むフェズの夜景。現在も中世の趣きを感じさせる光景である。

22-26: *Le Grand Visir*, one of 10 suites, contains an entrance space, drawing room, library, bedroom, bathroom and large veranda. Elaborate wood carvings adorn the ceiling of the sitting room. 27: The veranda of this suite looks out over the new market area of Fez. Even today, the scenery evokes much of the feeling of the Middle Ages.

23

24

100——Hotel Palais Jamai

25

26

27

Great Hotels of the World: vol. 4 —— 101

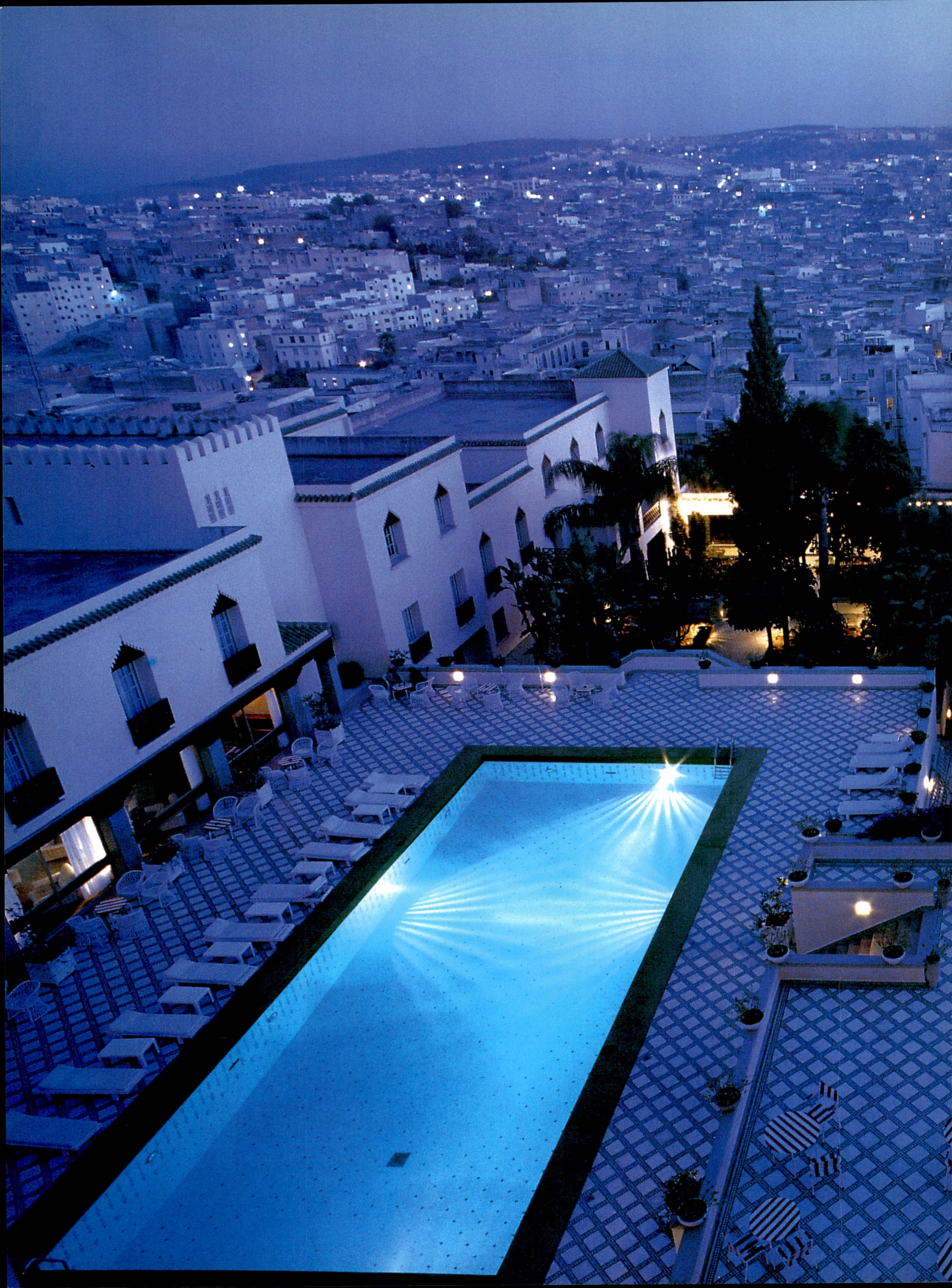

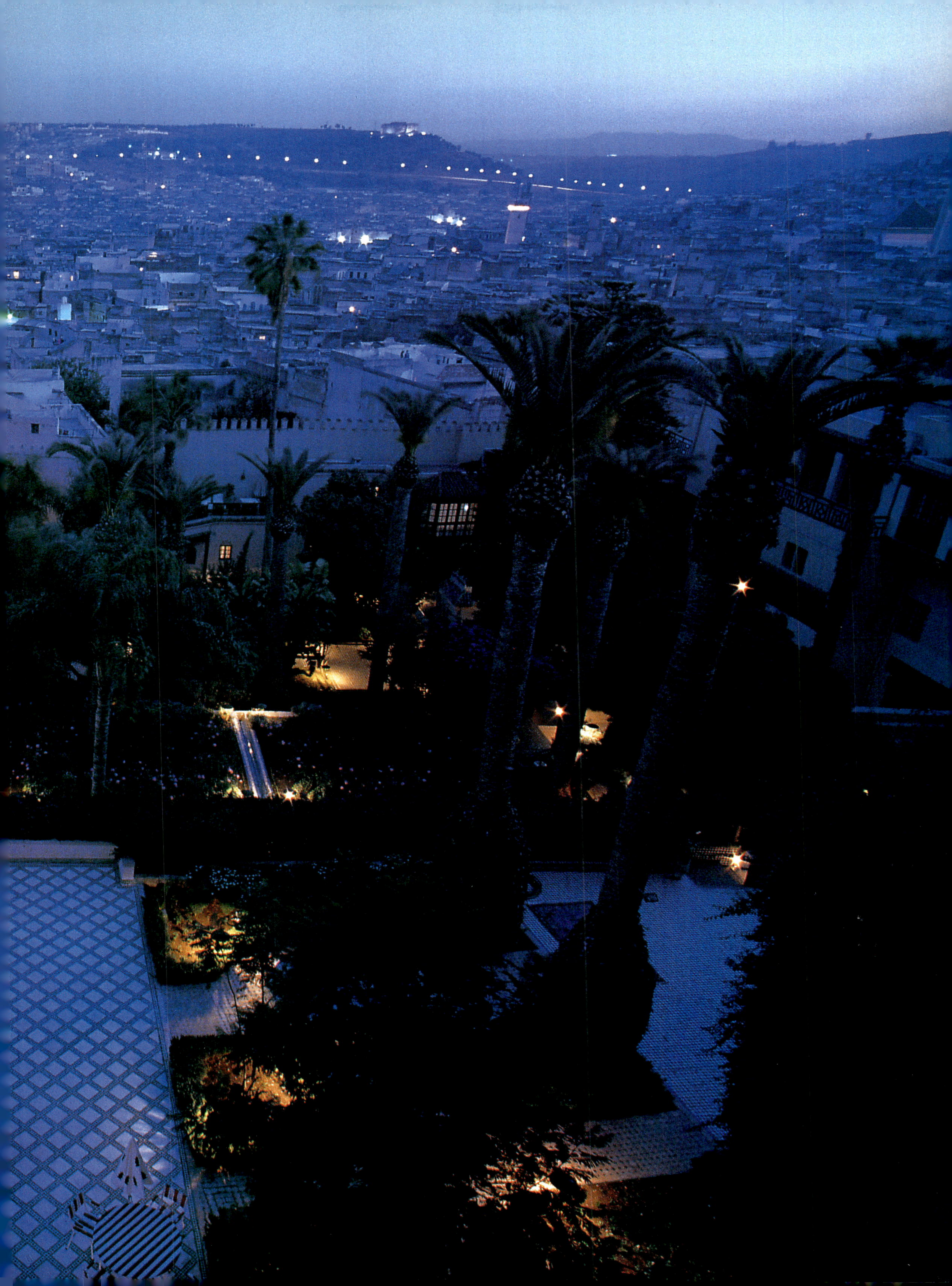

Hotel Byblos Andaluz
Mijas Galf, Mijas, Apt. 138 Fuengirola, Malaga, Spain

　地中海に面した南スペインの海岸地域は、コスタ・デル・ソル(太陽海岸)と呼ばれるリゾート地帯。近年、盛んに不動産投資(住宅、コンドミニアム、ホテルなど)が行なわれ、いまや近代的なアーバン・リゾート(都市とリゾートを融合させた地域)に姿を変えている。コスタ・デル・ソルの中心都市マラガから西方30kmの内陸に、1986年5月に開業したのがホテル・ビブロス・アンダルスである。

　アンダルシアのホテルにふさわしく、アラブ調の装飾で飾られ、パティオ(中庭)を囲む5階建の白いホテルで、フランス人の建築家オーヴリニョンとシキャルドンが構想を練り、スペイン人建築家ドン・マヌエル・シエラが建築を担当。スペインのホテルとしては珍しい海水と海藻を使ったボディ・トリートメント施設(タラソテラピー・インスティチュート)と36ホールのゴルフ場を付帯した新機軸のアーバン・リゾート・ホテルである。

●●●

On the coast along the Mediterranean in the south of Spain is the popular resort area known as the Costa del Sol ("Sun Coast"). In recent years, with extensive investment in residences, condominiums and hotels, the area has become a modern urban resort area, a fusion of resort facilities and urban amenities. Some 30 kilometers inland (westward) from Costa del Sol's capital city of Malaga, the gleaming white, five-story Hotel Byblos Andaluz was completed in May, 1986.

Befitting an Andalusian hotel, the interior courtyard and decorations are Arabic in style. The hotel was designed by French architects Auvrignon and Sicardon and was built by Spanish architect Don Manuel Sierra. An unusual feature is the "Thalassotherapy Institute," a "body treatment" facility which uses seawater and seaweed in its treatments. This pace-setting urban resort hotel also includes a 36-hole golf course.

1–3: ロバート・トレント・ジョーンズ設計による36ホールのゴルフ・コースがホテルを囲む。ホテルには真水を使った2つの屋外プール、5面のテニス・コートが設けられている。年間330日が晴天日と言う恵まれた環境にある。4:「レセプション」奥にあるアンダルシア風の噴水を置いた「ロビー」。

●●●

1–3: The hotel is surrounded by a 36-hole golf course designed by Robert Trent Jones. Facilities also include two fresh-water pools and five tennis courts. The area is blessed with excellent weather, with clear skies an average of 330 days each year. 4: An Andalusian-style fountain sits in one corner of the lobby reception area.

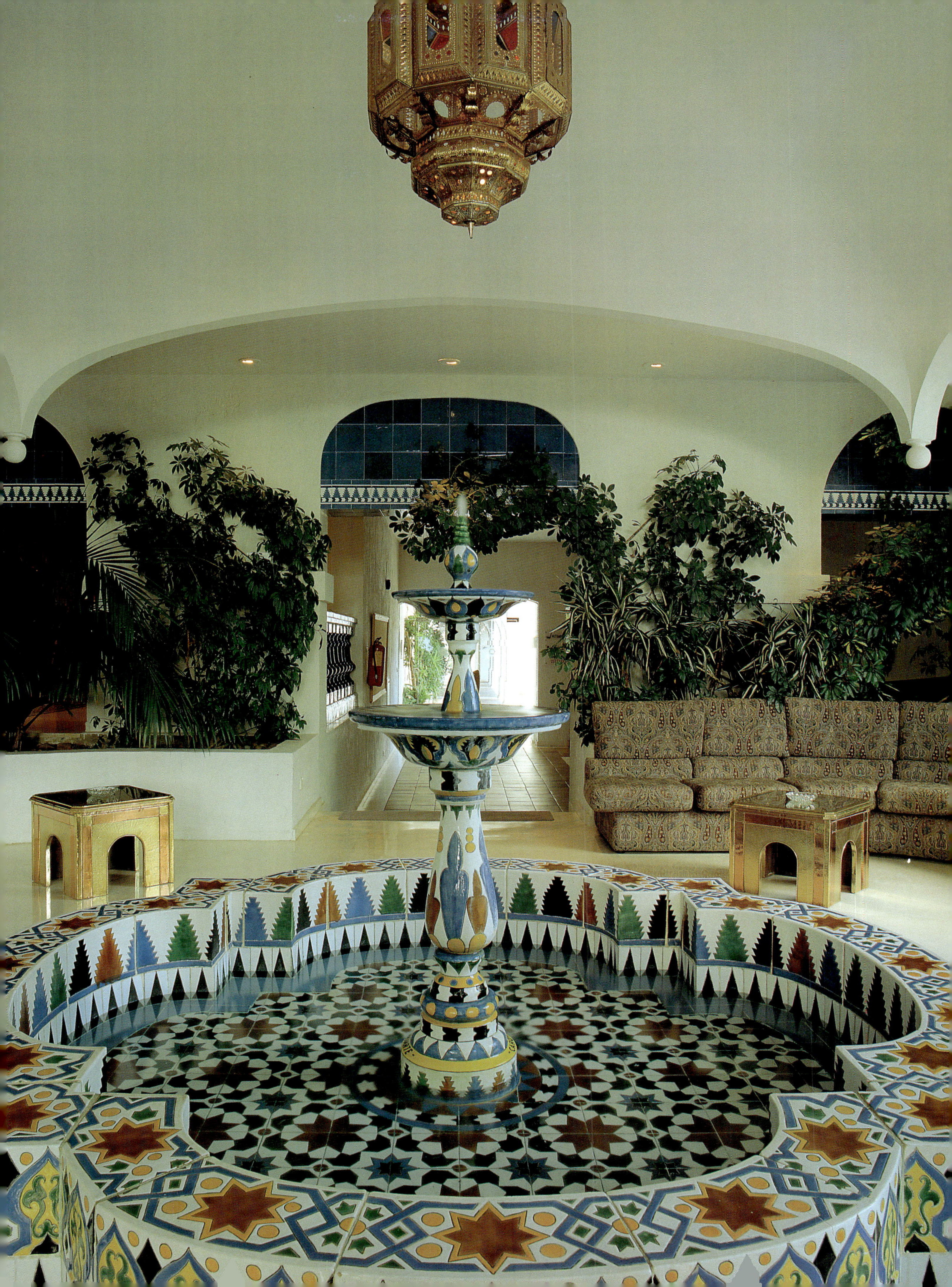

5
6
7
8

5,6: 大きなホテル・ロゴが床にデザインされた「レセプション」。7,8:「サン・トロペ・バー」はカウンター・スペースと2つの部屋から成る。9-11: フランス人シェフが美食料理を提供する「ル・ナヤック」。ディナー専用のレストランで、内装には煉瓦のアーチとタイルが使われている。席数60。食器は、アヴィランドのリモージュ焼き。

5, 6: The hotel logo is incorporated into the design of the floor in the reception area. 7, 8: The *St. Tropez Bar* consists of two separate rooms and a bar area. 9-11: *Le Nailhac* restaurant serves gourmet cuisine prepared by a French chef, and is open only for dinner. The Andalusian-style decor features brick arches and tilework, and up to 60 patrons can be accommodated. The servingware is Limoges porcelain by Haviland.

12
13

14

15
16

12: 宿泊棟から見たレストラン「エル・アンダルス」。プール・サイドのテラスで昼食を提供する。地元の魚貝類を使ったアンダルシア料理がビュッフェ形式で提供される。レストラン屋内部分には噴水のあるパティオが設けられ、1日分合計1,200カロリーのダイエット料理も用意されている。**13-16**: 水が流れる円形のパティオを囲む宿泊棟のひとつ。1階には多目的に利用できる多くの「サロン」がある。写真13は「サロン・グラナダ」で、アンダルシア様式の内装を取り入れている。

12: Located on the poolside terrace, facing the guest room wing, is *El Andaluz* restaurant, which serves lunch. Locally caught seafood is featured in the Andalusian-style buffet luncheon. The restaurant also offers a dietetic menu of dishes totalling 1,200 calories per day. The indoor area features a patio with a fountain. **13–16**: One of the guest room wings, built around a circular patio with water flow. A number of multi-purpose "salons" are located on the first-floor level. The *Salon Granada*, with Andalusian-style decor, is shown in photo no. 13.

17

17-19: ゴルフ・コースを一望する「ロイヤル・スイート」。20,21: テラスに屋根つきの休息スペースを持つ「プレジデンシャル・スイート」。応接間の壁を陶タイルで飾った独特の色調のスイートである。

17-19: The *Poyal Suite* offers a sweeping view of the golf course. **20, 21:** The terrace of the *Presidential Suite* includes a roofed rest area, and the drawing room walls are covered in glazed tile.

18 19

110——Hotel Byblos Andaluz

20

21

112 —— Hotel Byblos Andaluz

26

27

22-28: ホテルに隣接するボディ・トリートメント施設「ザ・ルイソン・ボベット・タラソテラピー・インスティテュート」。計7コースのうち数コースは、海藻パウダーと海水を使う健康回復治療法（写真25）。総面積2,500㎡。治療前に医師との面談がある。

●●●

22-28: *The Louison Bobet Thalassotherapy Institute* body treatment facility adjoining the hotel has an area of 2,500 square meters (27,000 square feet). Some of the facility's programs use powdered seaweed and seawater as part of a health restoration regimen (photo no. 25). Clients consult with a doctor before treatment begins.

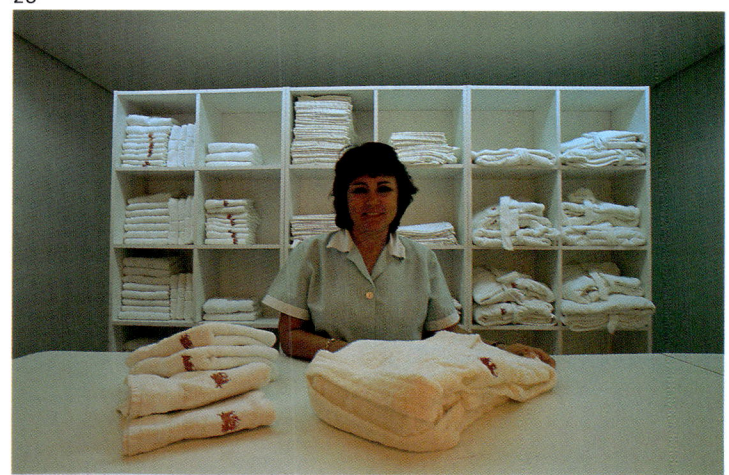

28

Ambasciatori Palace Hotel
Via V. Veneto 70, 00187 Rome, Italy

　半楕円形の古代ローマの遺跡コロッセオを彷彿とさせるホテルとして名高い。ミラノの実業家ジーノ・クレーリチがヴィットーリオ・ヴェーネト通りに建設した。建築家はマルチェッロ・ピアチェンティーニ。ラウンジと主要室には、ヴェネチアの著名な画家グイド・カドリンが多数のフレスコ画を描き、鍍金もまばゆいアンピール様式やシックでモダンなアール・デコ様式を取り入れた美しいホテルが1927年に開業。たちまち各国の大使が集うローマを代表するホテルとなった。

　その後、数回の改装でオリジナルな装飾は変更されてしまったが、30年代の上流階級のパーティやダンスの光景を描いたラウンジのフレスコ壁画は保存されており、開業期の華やかさを伝えている。

●●●

The Ambasciatori Palace Hotel is known for its close resemblance to the exterior of the ancient Roman Colosseum, completed in 80 BC. It was built halfway along the Via Vittorio Veneto, a winding, one-kilometer-long tree-lined avenue, by Milanese industrialist Gino Clerici.

The hotel was designed by architect Marcello Piacentini. The lounge and guest rooms are decorated with numerous fresco paintings by Venetian artist Guido Cadorin. The interior, which was completed in 1927, is known for its lavish Empire-style and Art Deco style decorations. In its early days the hotel was a favorite of ambassadors from various countries who were visiting Rome. Since that time it has been remodeled a number of times, and the original decor hardly remains. Fortunately, however, the original fresco paintings in the lounge, depicting the parties and dances of the aristocracy of the 1930's, have been preserved, and the hotel now stands as a reminder of the free-wheeling era in which it was built.

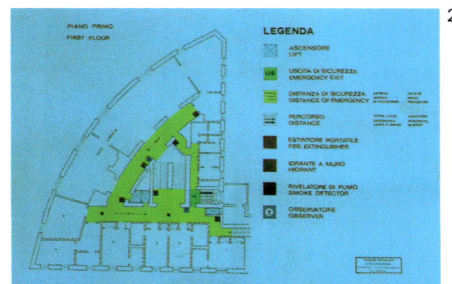

1: アメリカ大使館屋上から見たホテル本館(撮影協力:アメリカ大使館)。開業時からホテルの屋上には古代ローマの彫像が10体並んでいた。現在も外観は当時と変わらない。2: このホテルは半楕円形の本館と裏手の宿泊棟から成る。本館2階につくられた宴会施設の見取図。3: 真鍮製回転ドアが使われているホテル入口。4: 天井や壁に貴重なフレスコ画が残る半楕円形の「ピアノ・ラウンジ」。コーナーに小型の酒場「エンバシー・バー」が置かれている。

●●●

1: A row of ten ancient Roman statues originally stood on the roof. The exterior of the hotel, shown here as seen from the roof of the American Embassy, has remained unchanged since that time. (Photo made with the cooperation of the American Embassy). 2: A floor plan of the second-floor banquet facilities in the main building. The hotel is made up of a semi-elliptical main building and a separate guest room wing in the rear. 3: The entrance features a brass revolving door. 4: The small, intimate *Embassy Bar* occupies a portion of the semi-elliptical *Piano Lounge*, and magnificent fresco paintings have been preserved on the ceiling and walls.

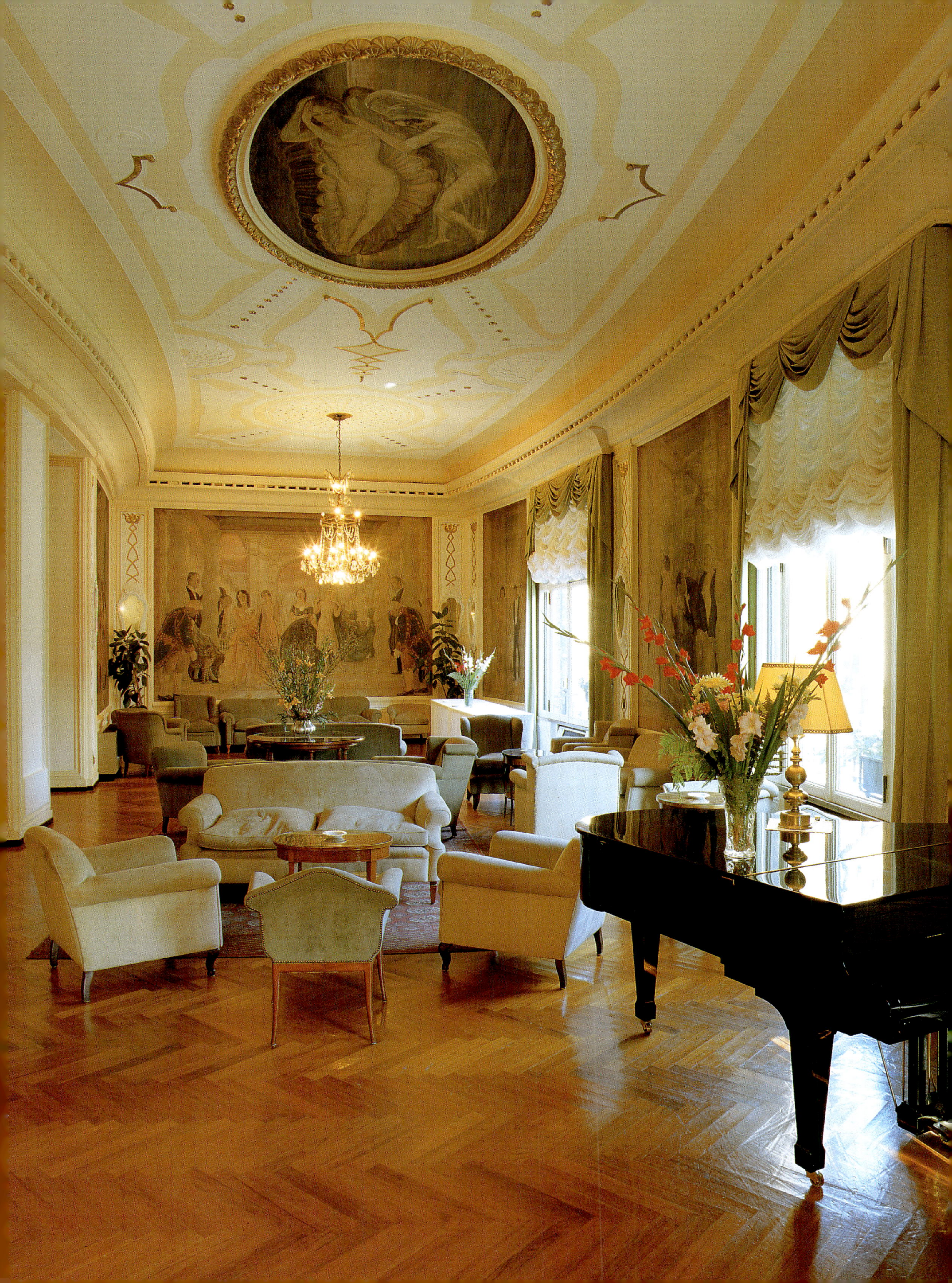

5

6 7

Ambasciatori Palace Hotel

5: 壁をテラコッタ装飾で飾った「レセプション」。6: 手作りの木製手摺子とニッチの彫像で飾られた階段。7,8: 建築家ピアチェンティーニが招いた画家カドリンが描いたフレスコの裸体画の一枚は以前はカーテンで隠されていた。アンティークの家具、クリスタル・シャンデリア、ヘリンボーン模様の寄木床を使った「ピアノ・ラウンジ」のコーナー部分。

5: Terra-cotta decorations cover the walls of the *Reception* area. 6: The staircase features hand-carved wooden handrails and statue-filled niches. 7, 8: One of the nude wall frescoes commissioned by architect Piacentini and painted by artist G. Cadorin was once hidden behind a curtain. Antique furniture, crystal chandeliers and a herringbone-patterned wooden floor add to the elegance of the *Piano Lounge*.

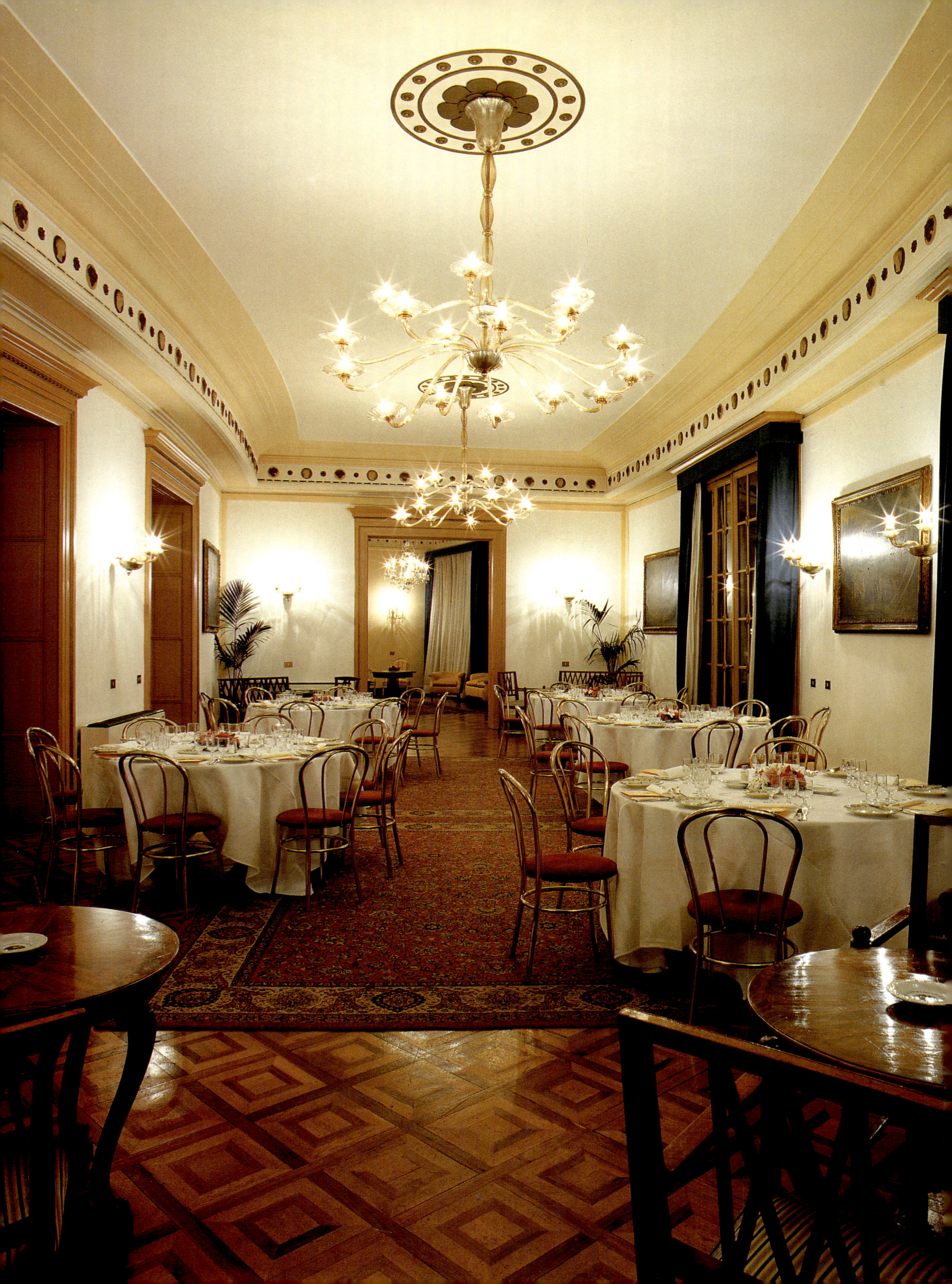

9-12: 本館2階には8つの宴会場、会議室が置かれ、10人から200人までのレセプションやバンケットに対応できる。最大の宴会場「サーラ・リンカーン」は「フォワイエ」が接続する設計。開業時の宴会場は、金色のアンピール様式の天井や壁で飾られ、アール・デコの装飾も取り入れられている。

9-12: Eight banquet rooms and a meeting room are on the second floor of the main building, and banquets and receptions of anywhere from ten to 200 guests can be accommodated. *Sala Lincoln*, the largest banquet room, adjoins the *Foyer*. When the banquet facilities first opened the walls and ceilings were decorated in Empire style, with additional Art Deco adornments.

13

14 15

120 ———— Ambasciatori Palace Hotel

16

17

13-15: 半地下階に置かれているイタリア料理の
レストラン「グリルABC（アビチ）」。同名のバーがレ
ストラン内部にある。昼食・夜食時にイタリアの代表
的なアンティパスト（前菜）がビュッフェ形式で提供
される。16-17: 以前は屋外テラスだった「ラ・テラ
ッツァ」。現在は屋根がかけられ、宿泊客用の朝食
レストランに改装された。昼は外来者のランチ・ミー
ティング（昼食会議）に使われる。

●●●

13-15: *Grill ABC*, the Italian restaurant on the basement mezzanine level, includes a bar of the same name. A buffet of typical Italian antipasto dishes is offered at lunchtime and dinner. 16, 17: *La Terrazza*, formerly an outdoor terrace, was roofed over and remodeled as a restaurant. It serves breakfast to hotel guests, and it is also available to the public for luncheon meetings.

18

20

19

122——Ambasciatori Palace Hotel

21

22

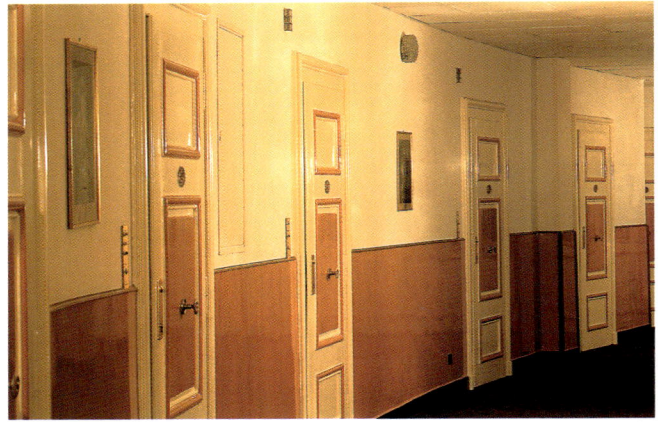

23

24

18-26: 14室あるスイートのひとつ「シニア・スイート」。本館に置かれ、応接間、寝室、浴室があり、他に一寝室を接続できる。半楕円形の廊下が保存され、開業時からの呼出しボタンが現在も使われている。バス・タブやトイレの排水口もシリンダー式のクラシックなもの。

18-26: The *Senior Suite* is one of 14 suites. Located in the main building, the suite consists of a drawing room, bedroom, and bath, with an additional bedroom that may be connected. The original curving hallways have been preserved, the original buttons used to call for service are still operational, and the original classic cylinder-style fixtures are still used in the suite's bathroom.

25

26

Great Hotels of the World: vol. 4 — 123

Hotel Metropole, Genève
34, Quai General Guisan CH-1204 Genève, Switzerland

　フランス・アルプスを望むレマン湖畔の都市ジュネーヴ。そのモンブラン橋のそばに4階建のホテル・メトロポールがある。開業は、1855年。〝グランド・ホテルの時代〟が初まる以前の時代である。設計はジュネーヴの建築家J・コラール。当時は、音楽家のワグナー、リスト、ベルリオーズなどが好んでこのホテルに泊ったという。1940〜41年には、国際赤十字委員会の要請でジュネーヴ市が費用を負担し、戦傷者用の病院として利用された。

　1975年12月31日にホテルは一時閉鎖され、近代設備を導入するための全面的改修工事が開始された。地域規制によって増築工事は見送られ、開業時のスケールのまま1982年11月22日にふたたび開業。新しいホテルは各階に休息スペースを持ち、最高のサービスを提供する小型ラクシャリー・ホテルとして特定の個人客が好んで利用している。

●●●

The city of Genève lies on the shores of Lac Leman (Lake Geneva), overlooking the French Alps. The four-story Hotel Metropole was built in Geneva back in 1855, in the days before the "Age of Grand Hotels," by local architect Joseph Collart. The hotel, which is on the lakeshore and near Geneva's Pont du Mont-Blanc, soon became popular with composers such as Richard Wagner, Franz Liszt and Hector Berlioz. In 1940–41, at the request of the International Committee of the Red Cross, it was used as a hospital to treat persons wounded in the war.

On New Year's Eve, 1975, it closed for complete renovation work and installation of modern facilities. Because of local regulations it could not be enlarged, so it reopened in November, 1982 in its original scale. The Hotel Metropole has gained a reputation among discriminating guests as a small-scale luxury hotel offering the highest quality of service.

1, 2: 最初のオーナーは、この付近の地主クリスチャン・フレデリック・コーラーだったが、開業前に所有権をホテル・メトロポール・カンパニーに譲渡し、現在はジュネーヴ市が所有。3: 開業時のホテル（イラスト提供：ホテル・メトロポール・ジュネーヴ）。4, 7: 2階に置かれたロビー・ラウンジ「ル・ホール」から見た「ザ・メイン・エントランス」。天井には青空を飛ぶ鳥、壁には仮面の道化師の画が、画家D．アッピアにより描かれた。

●●●

1, 2: The hotel's original owner was a neighborhood landowner, Christian Frederic Kohler; however, ownership was transferred to the Hotel Metropole Company before it opened. The present owner is the city of Genève. 3: The hotel as it appeared when it first opened. (Illustration courtesy of Hotel Metropole Genève). 4, 7: View of *The Main Entrance* from the second-floor lounge, *Le Hall*. The ceiling mural depicts birds flying in a blue sky, and the walls are covered with paintings of harlequins done by painter D. Appia.

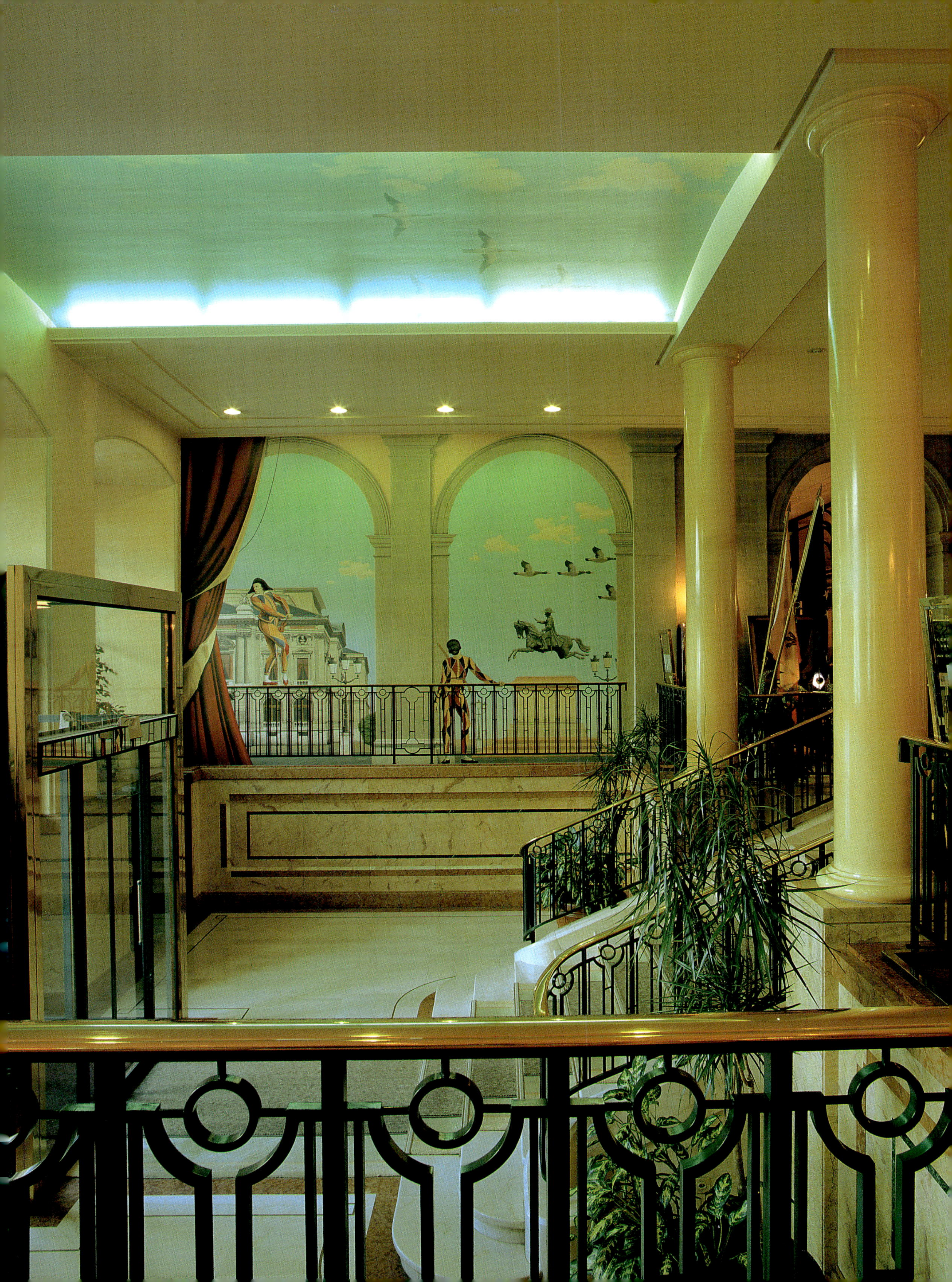

Hotel Metropole, Genève

5,6: ロビー・ラウンジ「ル・ホール」の奥には、カウンターのある「ル・バール」が置かれている。「ル・ホール」は、アフタヌーン・ティーやカクテル・パーティーにも使われる。8: 2階に設けられた「レセプション」。9-11:「レセプション」裏に位置する「ル・グラン・ケー(大波止場)」。中央階段下部の入口は外来者用として使われる。1階に「ブラスリー」もあり、夏期には戸外レストランもオープンする。

5, 6: *Le Bar* is located in a corner of *Le Hall* lobby lounge. *Le Hall* is also used for cocktail parties and afternoon tea. 8: The second-floor *Reception* area. 9-11: Behind the *Reception* is *Le Grand Quai* ("The Big Wharf"). The entrance at the bottom of the central staircase is used by visitors. A *Brasserie* is located on the first floor, and in the summer an outdoor restaurant opens.

Great Hotels of the World: vol. 4

12

13

12, 13: ホテルのメイン・ダイニング「ラルルカン」。パントマイムの人気者、仮面の道化師（アルルカン）から命名されたフランス料理のレストラン。14, 15: 各階には大きなスペースを持つ「シッテイング・エリア」が2ヶ所設けられている。16:「ルーム・サービス」のスタッフ。このホテルの最上階（5階）には「コンフェランス・ルーム」が置かれ、夏には屋上に日光浴用のテラスが設けられる。

12, 13: *L'Arlequin,* the hotel's main dining room, takes its name from the French word for "harlequin." French food is served. 14, 15: Each floor has two large *Sitting Areas.* 16: The room service staff. A *Conference Room* is located on the top floor, and the roof has a sunbathing terrace for use in summer.

128——Hotel Metropole, Genève

14

15

16

130——Hotel Metropole, Genève

19

17,18: レマン湖やモンブラン橋を見渡す「ジュニア・スイート」。玄関スペースにワードローブを置き、応接間、寝室、浴室で構成される。朝食の「ルーム・サービス」のセッテイング。ホテル全室にビデオ再生装置があり、「レセプション」からのレンタルも可能。19-21:最高級の部屋「デラックス・スイート」。

17, 18: The *Junior Suite*, with views of Lake Geneva and Pont du Mont-Blanc, includes an entrance area with wardrobe, drawing room, bedroom and bath. A breakfast setting from room service is shown. Each guest room includes a video player, and rental tapes are available from the reception desk. 19–21: The top-class *Deluxe Suite*.

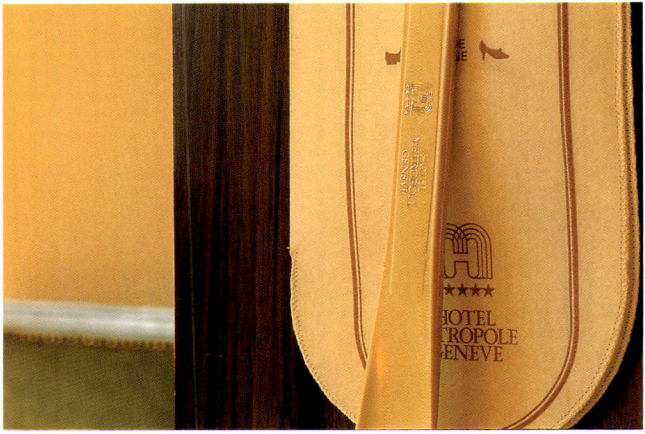

20

21

Atlantic Hotel Kempinski Hamburg
An der Alster 72, D-2000 Hamburg 1, Germany

　ドイツ最大の貿易港ハンブルクのアウセンアルスター湖畔に立つ白亜のホテル。その美しい姿から〝町の真珠〟とも呼ばれている。1907年、ベルリン・ホテル協会によって建設を開始、1909年5月2日に開業。当時、大西洋航路に就航していた豪華客船インペラートア号とオイローパ号の一等客船のために開発されたことから「アトランティック・ホテル」と命名された。

　皇帝ヴィルヘルム2世の時代に開業したため、内装はヴィルヘルム様式。開業時の総室数は250室。そのうち100室には専用のバス・ルームが付設され、全室に暖房装置・水道・電話など、当時としては画期的な近代設備が採用された。第2次世界大戦後の1954年、ホテルはケンピンスキー・グループ（ドイツのホテル会社）の傘下に入り、豪華客船時代が終わった現在においても、世界の一流のゲストたちに愛されつづけている。

●●●

This chalk-white hotel stands on the shores of Aussenalster Lake in Hamburg, Germany's largest trading port. Because of its striking appearance it was nicknamed the "Pearl of the City." The Berlin Hotel Association began construction in 1907, finishing in May 1909. The hotel was developed to cater to passengers crossing the Atlantic on luxury liners such as the newly commissioned *Imperator* and *Europa*, and so it was named the Atlantic Hotel.

Since the hotel opened during the reign of Kaiser Wilhelm II, the interior is done in "Wilhelmian style." Of the 250 guest rooms, some 100 had their own bathrooms, and all rooms were equipped with such modern facilities as heating units, running water and telephones, a revolutionary advancement for that era. In 1954 the hotel was acquired by the Kempinski Group, a German hotel management company. Even today, long after the era of luxury passenger ships, this first-class hotel remains beloved by its loyal guests from around the world.

1-3：当時1,400万ライヒス・マルクを投じて建設された〝白い城〟の別名も持つホテル。第2次世界大戦後の5年間、英国軍に接収された歴史を持つ。4：「グローサー・ザール（大広間）」とも呼ばれる大宴会場「ザ・グランド・ボールルーム」。レセプション形式で600名、バンケット形式で320名を収容。総面積364㎡。かつては世界の王族、貴族、政治家たちが参集した。

●●●

1-3: The Atlantic Hotel, also nicknamed the "White Castle," was built at a cost of 14 million Reichsmarks. After World War II it was requisitioned by the British army for five years. 4: *The Grand Ballroom* banquet area, with a total area of 364 square meters (3,900 sq. ft.), has a capacity of 600 for receptions and 320 for banquet-style events. It was once a gathering place for royalty and government officials from around the world.

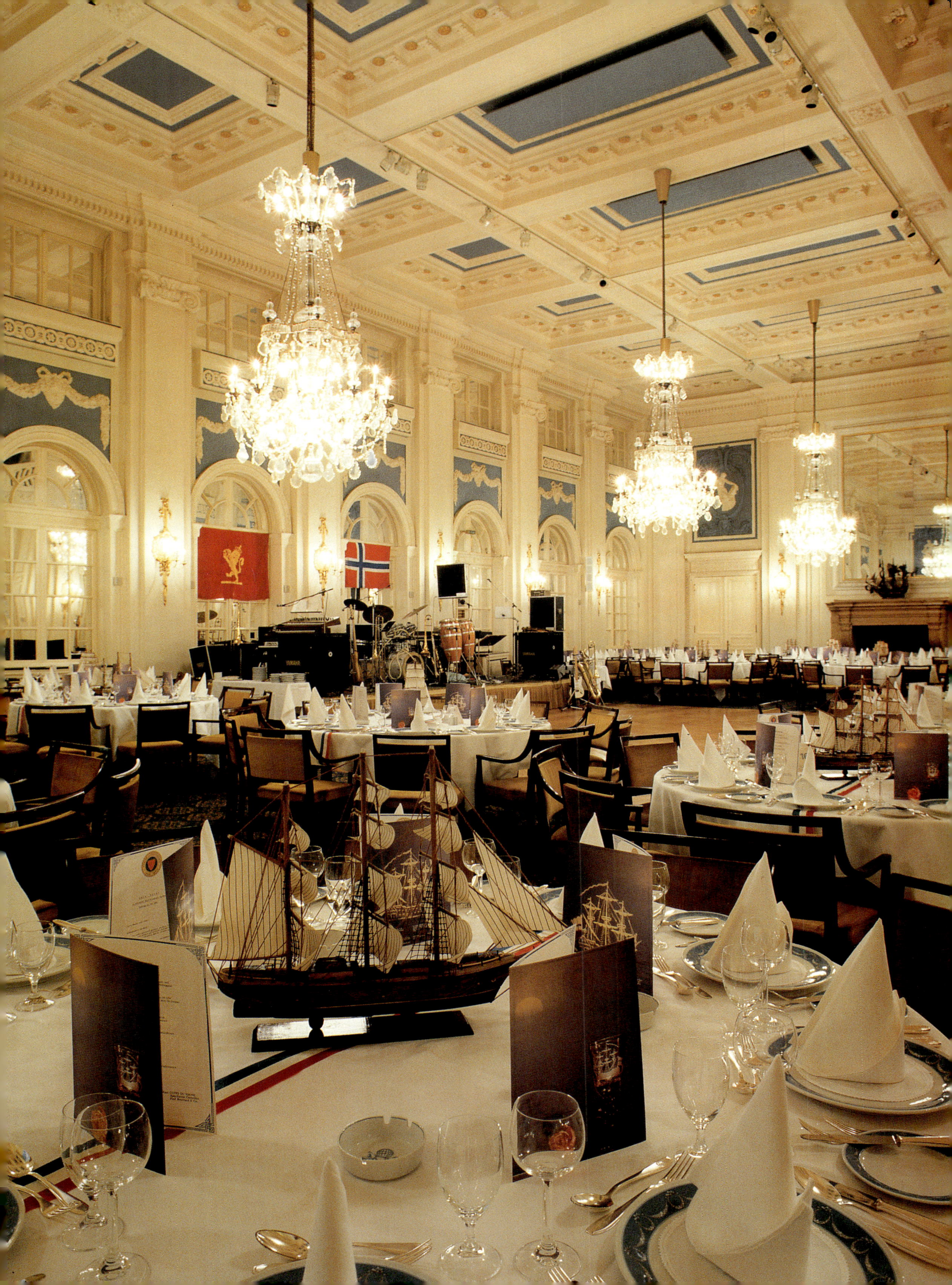

5: 玄関大広間「アトランティック・ホール」奥のシッティング・スペース。壁を飾る肖像画はカイザー・ヴィルヘルム2世。6:「アトランティック・ホール」横にある「バー・アトランティック」。7: 新フランス料理と地元ハンザ料理を提供するメイン・ダイニング「アトランティック・グリル」。窓側にテラス・スペースがある。8: 大小16室ある宴会場のひとつ「ヴァイサー・ザール・(白の間)」。9: 各階段の上下にも広いスペースを取り、デスクやソファーが置かれている。

●●●

5: A sitting area at the back of the enormous *Atlantic Hall*. On the wall is a portrait of Kaiser Wilhelm II. 6: The *Bar Atlantic* is next to the *Atlantic Hall*. 7: The *Atlantic Grill* main dining room serves French *nouvelle cuisine* and local Hanseatic dishes, and includes a terrace area. 8: The *Weisser Saal* ("White Room") is one of 16 banquet rooms of various sizes. 9: Desks and sofas occupy the large landings of each stairway.

7

8

9

Great Hotels of the World: vol. 4 ——— 135

10
12
11

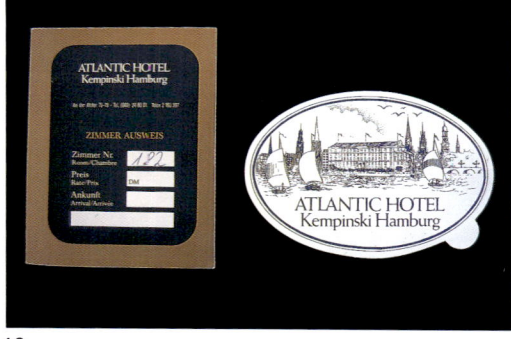

10, 11: 応接間、寝室、浴室より成る「スイート・ルーム」。クラシックなムードにリノヴェーションされている。**12**: レジストレーション・カードとステッカー。**13, 14**: 応接間と寝室をカーテンで分けた「スイート・ルーム」。近年、3,000万マルクをかけてリノヴェーションを完了。420名の従業員と数十名の実習生が温かくもてなしてくれるホテルとして世界に知られている。

●●●

10, 11: This *Suite*, renovated and redecorated in classical style, includes a drawing room, bedroom and bathroom. **12**: A reception card and sticker. **13, 14**: The drawing room and bedroom are separated by a curtain in this *Suite*. Renovation work totalling 30 million Marks was recently completed. With 420 employees and numerous trainees, the hotel is known around the world for the warm, friendly service it provides.

136 —— Atlantic Hotel Kempinski Hamburg

13
14

Hotel Metropole, Brussels
31, Place de Brouckere, B-1000 Brussels, Belgium

　ベルギーの首都ブリュッセルを代表する初期のグランド・ホテルのひとつ。創業者は飲食業で成功をおさめたウィルマンス家のクーペンスで、開業は1895年。建築家はデコレーターとしても名高かったアルバン・シャンボン。シャンボンはフランス・ルネサンス様式の内装を採用し、さらに採光を多数のステンド・グラスからとる方式をとった。

　1911年に物理学者ソルヴェイ主催による会議が開かれて、キュリー夫人、アインシュタインなどが参加し、一躍このホテルの名が世界に知られることになった。その後、増改築が行なわれたが、一階の大通路、一階天井を飾るシャンデリア、会議室は開業時の内装を今も保っている。現在もウィルマンス家4代目当主がホテルを所有しており、各室のリノヴェーションを慎重に進めている。

The Hotel Metropole, which opened in 1895 in the Belgian capital of Brussels, is typical of early Grand Hotels. Its founder, Mr. Ceuppens of the Belgian Wielemans family, was a successful entrepreneur in the food and drink industry. The architect, Alban Chambon, was a famous decorator, and in the hotel he created a French Early Renaissance style interior lit by numerous stained glass windows.

In 1911 the hotel was catapulted to worldwide fame after it played host to an international physics conference, organized by Belgian physicist Ernest Solvay and attended by Marie Curie, Albert Einstein and other celebrated scientists. Soon afterward the hotel underwent renovation and expansion work; however, the original first-floor hallway, first-floor chandeliers and meeting room interior decor have been preserved. The present owner is a member of the fourth generation from the Wielemans family, and discreet renovation work on the guest rooms is currently underway.

1,3：ブリュッセル市の商店街ブルッケール広場に立つホテル。2：開業時のホテル全景（写真提供：ホテル・メトロポール）。4：「レセプション・ルーム」横の美しい宴会場「アルトゥール・ルービンシュタイン・ルーム」。チュニジア産のピンク・ブラウン大理石とステンド・グラスで飾られ、開業時から約100年間使用されている大クリスタル・シャンデリアはベルギーの〝ヴァル・サン・ランベール〟社製。この宴会場と「エントランス・ホール」、「レセプション・ルーム」の天井は、〝ロワールのシャトー群〟を想起させる初期ルネサンスの様式。

1, 3: The hotel is located in the Brouckere plaza shopping district of Brussels. 2: A view of the hotel at the time of its opening. (Photo courtesy of Hotel Metropole). 4: The beautiful *Arthur Rubinstein Room*, a banquet room next to the *Reception Poom*, features stained glass windows and pink and brown Tunisian marble. The large crystal chandeliers, made by the famous Belgian firm of Val Saint Lambert, have been in use for nearly 100 years, since the hotel first opened. This banquet room, the *Entrance Hall* and the ceiling of the *Reception Room* are all decorated in an Early Renaissance style reminiscent of the *chateaux* of the Loire.

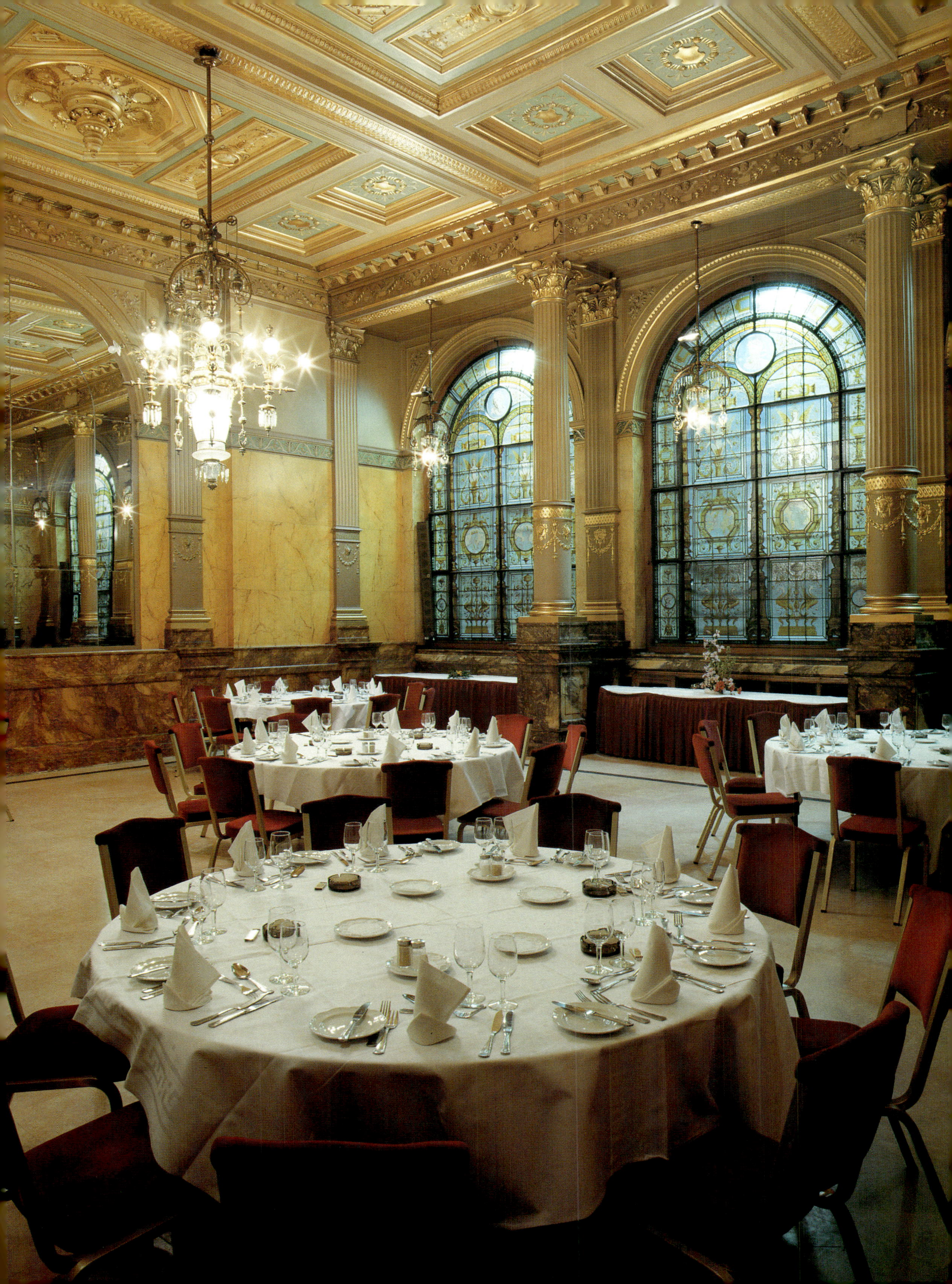

5,7:「レセプション・ルーム」とキー・ラック。6,8:「レセプション・ルーム」前の「エントランス・ホール」。中央奥が「ラ・ディズヌーヴィエム・バール（19世紀バー）」、左側が「レセプション・ルーム」、右側に入口（写真:8）と「カフェ・メトロポール」がある。9:「19世紀バー」は開業時のサロン「ジャルダン・ディヴェール（冬の庭園）」を改装したもの。10: ベル・エポックの昔から著名人に愛され続けている「カフェ・メトロポール」。

●●●

5, 7: The *Receotion Room* and a key rack. **6, 8**: In front of the *Reception Room* is the *Entrance Hall*. To the center rear is *La 19ième Bar*, to the left is the *Reception Room*, and to the right is the entrance (photo no. 8) and the *Cafe Metropole*. **9**: The original *Jardin d'Hiver* ("Winter Garden") was remodeled as *La 19ième Bar*. **10**: *Cafe Metropole* has been a favorite gathering place for celebrities since the long-ago days of the Belle Epoque.

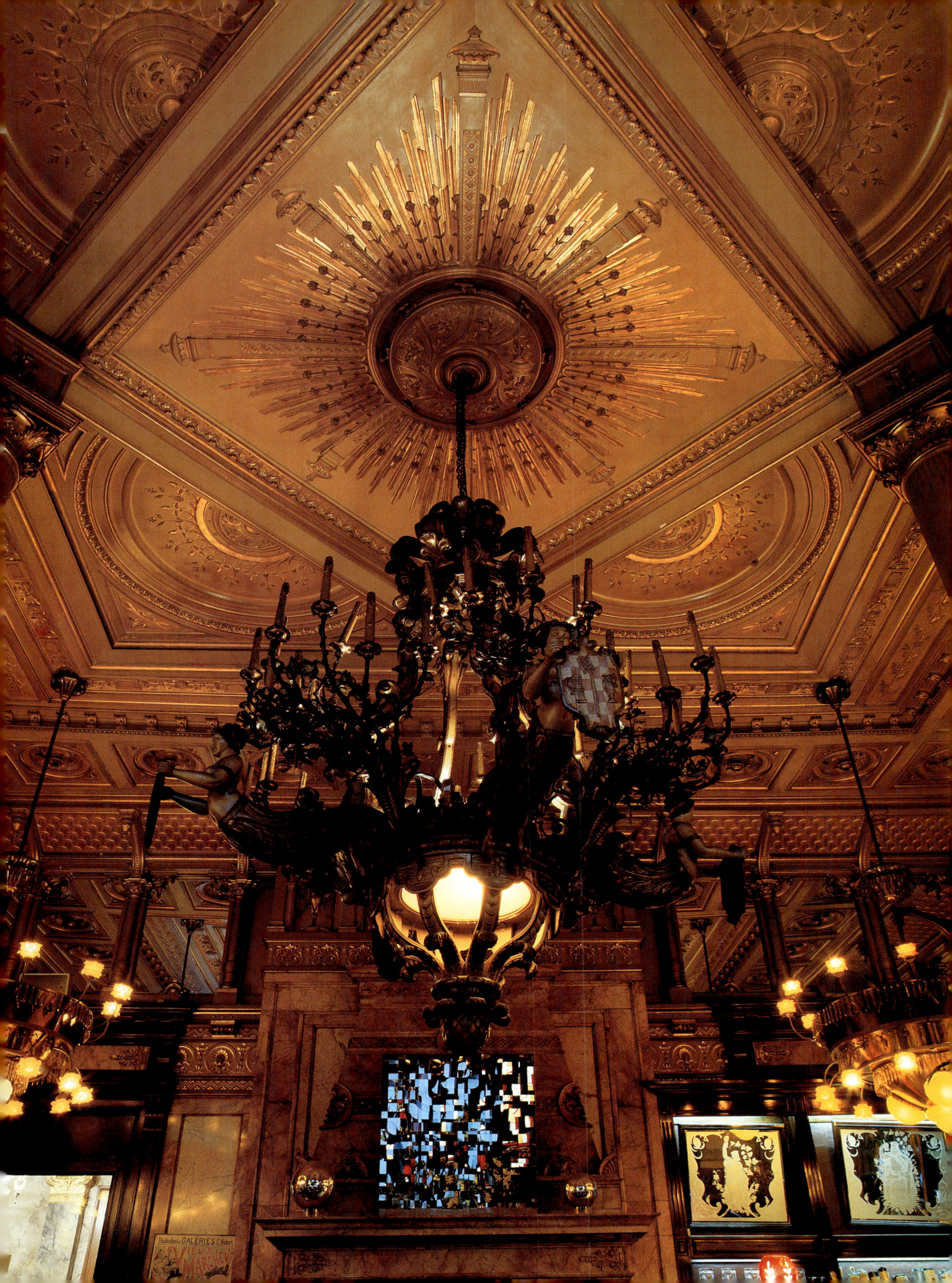
GALERIES

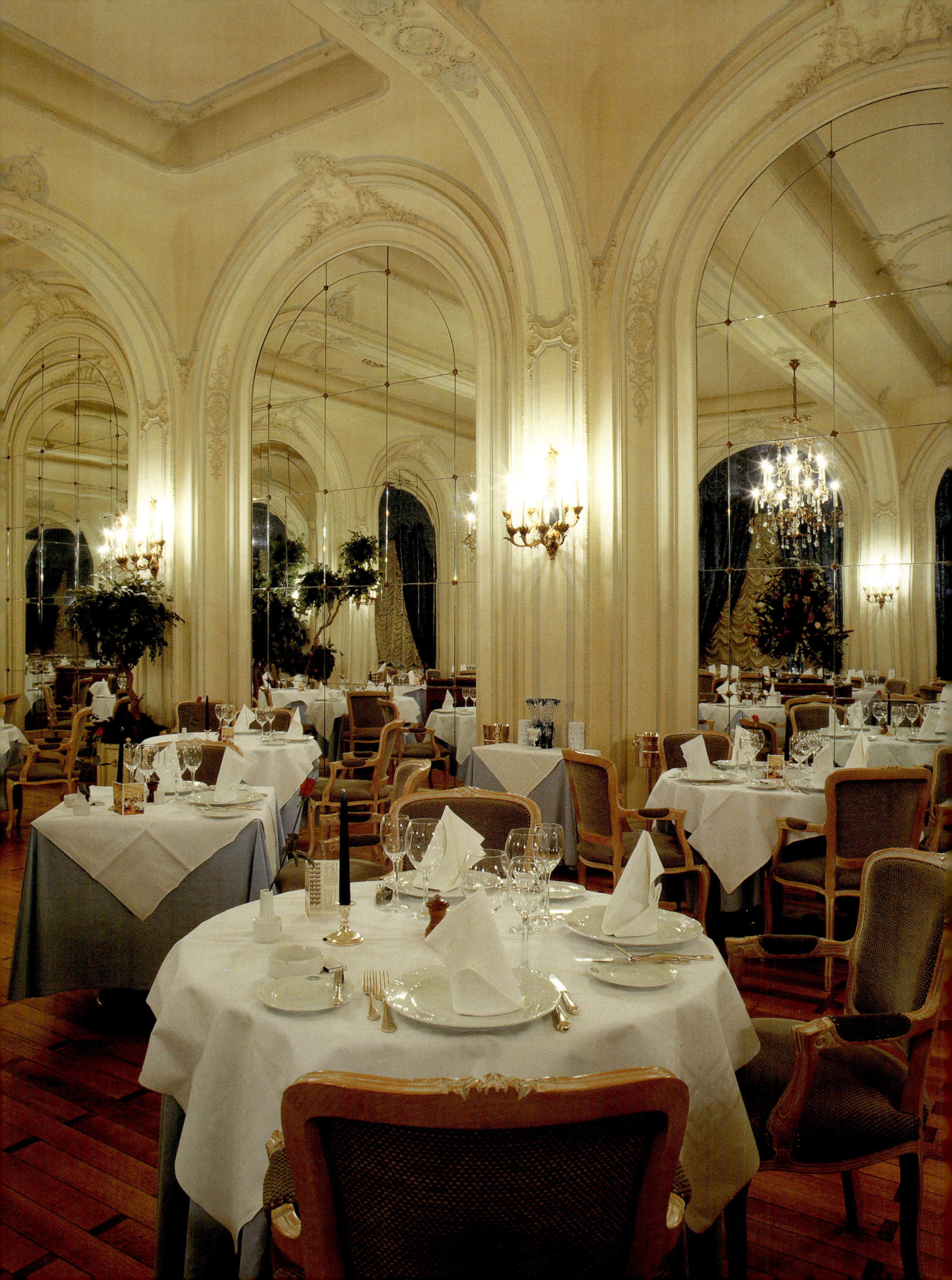

11:ホテルの建築家の名を冠したメイン・ダイニング「ラルバン・シャンボン・レストラン」。12:パリのエッフェル塔と同じメーカーの古いフランス製エレヴェーターが1基使われている。13:各階の廊下に置かれたデスクの飾り。14:物理学者キュリー夫人の名をつけた会議室「マリー・キュリー・ルーム」。15:1911年に開催された"世界物理学者会議"の記念写真(写真提供:ホテル・メトロポール)。前列左から3人目が主催者のソルヴェイ、8人目がキュリー夫人、後列右から2人目がアインシュタイン。その後のリノヴェーションのため、写真の会議室は現存しない。

●●●

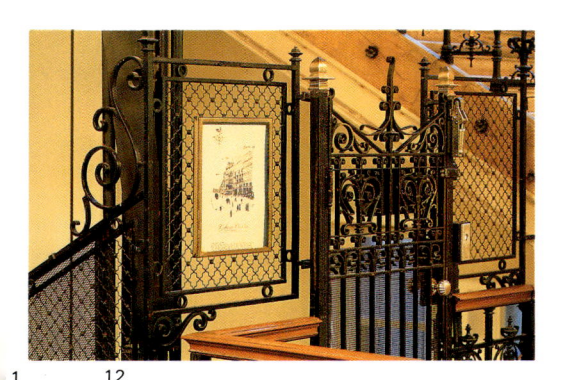

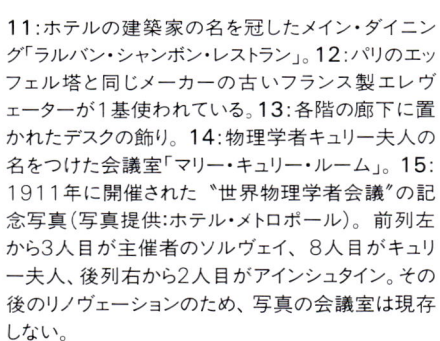

11: *L'Alban Chambon Restaurant*, the main dining room, is named after the hotel's architect. 12: An antique elevator manufactured by the same French company that built the Eiffel Tower. 13: Desks stand in the hallways on each floor. 14: The *Marie Curie Room* is a meeting room named after the famous scientist. 15: A commemorative photograph of the 1911 international physics conference. (Photo courtesy of Hotel Metropole). In the front row, third from the left, is conference organizer Solvay, and eighth from the left is Marie Curie. Einstein is second from the right in the back row. Because of subsequent renovation work, the meeting room shown here no longer exists.

Great Hotels of the World: vol. 4 — 143

16, 17:最高級の部屋「プレジデンシャル・スイート」。応接間、寝室、ワードローブ室、浴室から構成されている。18-21:新装された「ジュニア・スイート」。なお宿泊者専用の朝食レストラン「サロン・アインシュタイン」は地下に設けられている。

16, 17: The top-class *Presidential Suite* includes a drawing room, bedroom, wardrobe room and bathroom. **18–21:** The newly redecorated *Junior Suite*. Breakfast is served to hotel guests in the basement-level *Salon Einstein*.

144 —— Hotel Metropole, Brussels

18

19

20

21

Great Hotels of the World: vol. 4 — 145

Selsdon Park Hotel
Sanderstead, South Croydon, Surrey, CR2 8YA, G. Britain

ロンドンの南に広がる美しい丘陵地セルスドンに立つ歴史的なホテル。17世紀のチャールズ2世時代にクリストファー・ボウヤーが建てた農家と農場が現在のホテルの基礎となっている。1809年、東インド会社の取締役もつとめた銀行家・政治家ジョージ・スミスが入手してネオ・ゴシック様式の邸宅に改築し、1877年までスミス家が所有。現エリザベス女王の母后はこのスミス家の出身である。その後、邸宅はいく人かの人手を経て、1923年に実業家のアラン・サンダーソンが買収し、1925年に23室の小ホテルとして開業。1927〜35年には建築家ヒュー・マッキントッシュにより両側にネオ・ジャコビアン様式の建物が増築された。

現在は敷地に18ホールのゴルフ場も付設され、のどかで荘重なたたずまいのお屋敷ホテルとして知られている。

●●●

This historic hotel stands in the beautiful hilly region of Selsdon, to the south of London. The present hotel was originally a farmhouse built by Christopher Bowyer in the 17th century, during the era of King Charles II. In 1809 the farmhouse was renovated in Neo-Gothic style by George Smith, a banker, politician, and director of the famous East India Company. It was used as the family mansion until 1877. (The present Queen Mother is a descendant of the Smith family).

The property then passed through a number of different hands, and in 1923 was bought by businessman Allan Sanderson. In 1925 it opened as a small, 23-room hotel, and between 1927 and 1935 new, Neo-Jacobean style additions were constructed on either side under the direction of architect Hugh Mackintosh. The present hotel includes an 18-hole golf course, and it is known as a quiet mansion-style hotel with a dignified, stately appearance.

1：ロンドンの南方20km、81万㎡の敷地にゴルフ場とホテルがある。2,3：1925年の最初のホテルの空中写真と19世紀初期「セルスドン・ハウス」と呼ばれた頃の絵（写真、イラスト提供：セルスドン・パーク・ホテル）。4：17世紀からのオリジナル天井が保存される広間「バー・ラウンジ」。天井のイニシャルI・R（現在のJ・R：ジェームズ・ロイヤルの意）は、17世紀初頭の英国王ジェームズ1世の紋章。

●●●

1: The hotel and golf course occupy an 810,000-square-meter (200-acre) site just 20 kilometers (13 miles) south of London. 2, 3: The first aerial photograph of the hotel, taken in 1925, and an early 19th-century illustration titled "Selsdon House." (Photo and illustration courtesy of Selsdon Park Hotel). 4: The original 17th-century ceiling has been preserved in the expansive *Bar Lounge*. The initials "I.R." ("J.R." in modern script) are part of the coat of arms of England's King James I, who ruled in the early 17th century.

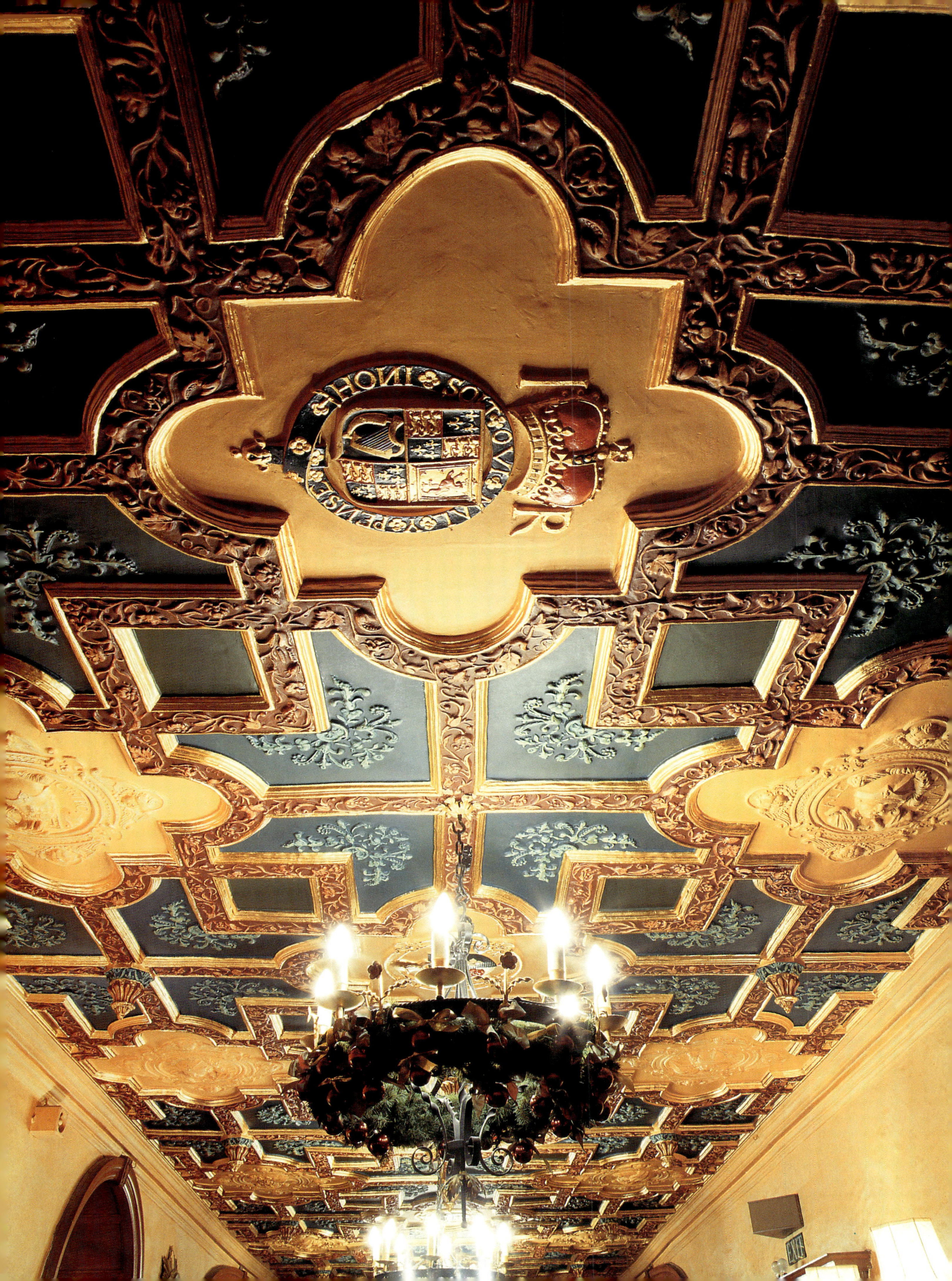

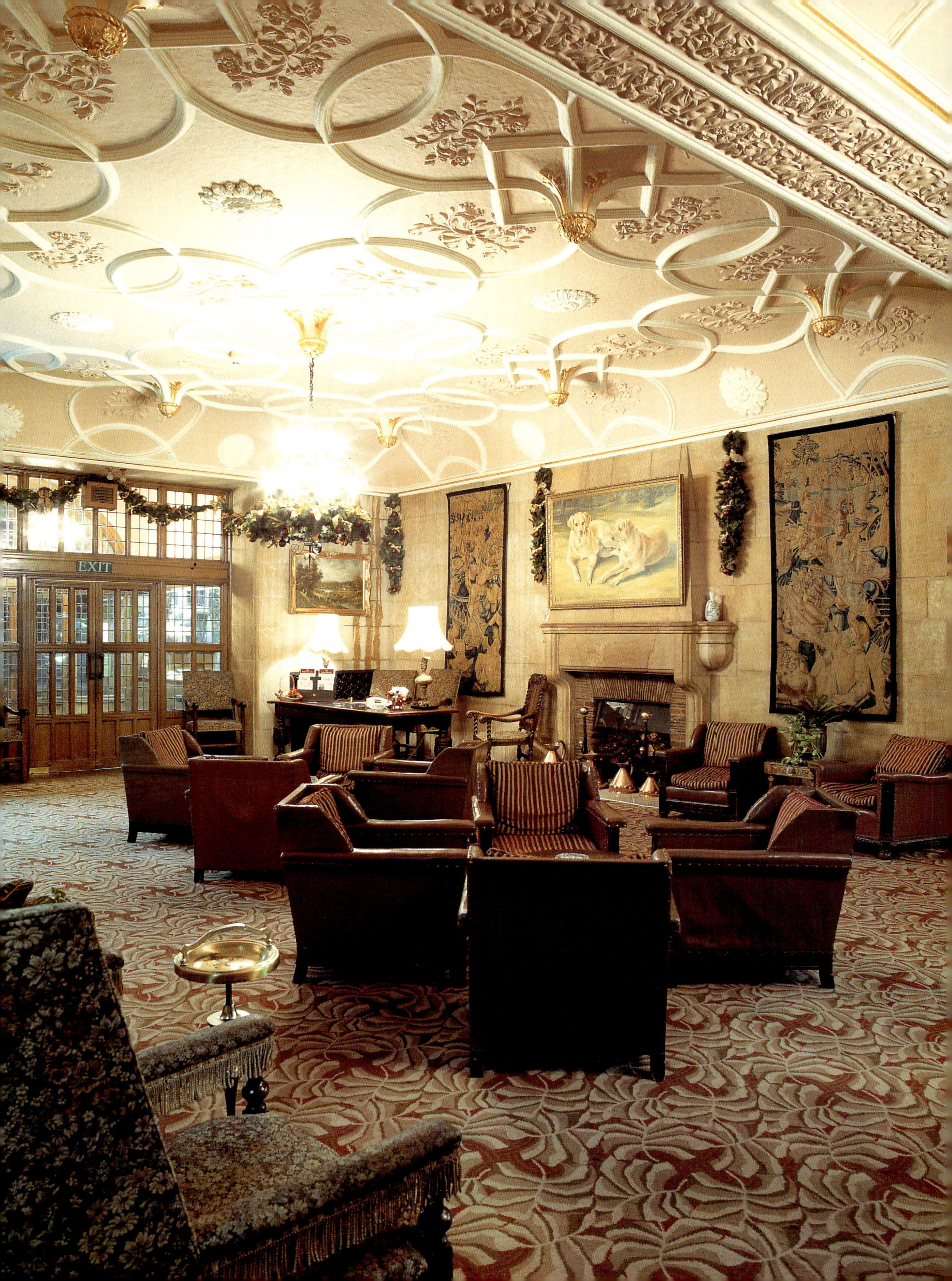
EXIT

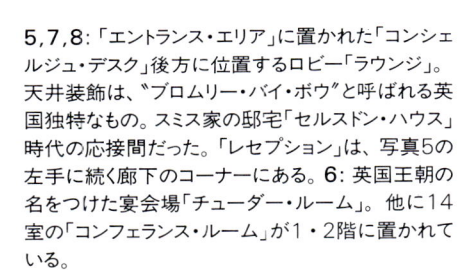

5,7,8:「エントランス・エリア」に置かれた「コンシェルジュ・デスク」後方に位置するロビー「ラウンジ」。天井装飾は、"ブロムリー・バイ・ボウ"と呼ばれる英国独特なもの。スミス家の邸宅「セルスドン・ハウス」時代の応接間だった。「レセプション」は、写真5の左手に続く廊下のコーナーにある。6: 英国王朝の名をつけた宴会場「チューダー・ルーム」。他に14室の「コンフェランス・ルーム」が1・2階に置かれている。

5, 7, 8: Behind the *Concierge Desk* in the *Entrance Area* is the lobby *Lounge*, with typically English "Bromley-by-bow" ceiling decorations. This area was used as the drawing room when the Smith family still lived in Selsdon House. (The *Reception Desk* is located further along the hallway visible on the left in photo no. 5). **6:** The *Tudor Room* banquet room is named after the English royal house of the same name. There are also 14 *Conference Rooms* on the first and second floors.

Great Hotels of the World: vol. 4 —— 149

9–11:「ラウンジ」と「バー・ラウンジ」の中間にある階段。古い置時計、ステンドクラス窓、木彫りのライオン、アンティーク・ライトなどで飾られている。
12: 唯一の近代的施設「ヘルス・クラブ」の屋内プール。プール中央のスペースでお茶が楽しめる。
13–15:「バー・ラウンジ」は、17世紀の天井が残され、当時流行したバルバス(球根状の飾り)を取り入れた賞杯棚が現在も置いてある。中央奥が、17世紀の木彫暖炉のあるアフタヌーン・ティー・コーナー。17世紀の装飾、家具がそのまま使われている貴重な部屋である。

●●●

9–11: Antique lighting fixtures, table clocks, wood carvings of lions and stained glass windows lend an air of antiquity to the stairway between the *Lounge* and the *Bar Lounge*. 12: The *Health Club* is equipped with modern facilities, including an indoor pool. Tea is served in an area near the middle of the pool. 13–15: A "bulbous" cupboard, popular in the 17th century, has been preserved in the *Bar Lounge* along with the original 17th-century ceiling. To the rear of the center is an original 17th-century carved wood fireplace, and afternoon tea is served nearby. The original decorations and furnishings preserved here add a special charm to this room.

150 —— Selsdon Park Hotel

13

14

15

Great Hotels of the World: vol.4 ——— 151

16

17
18

152——Selsdon Park Hotel

19

20

16–18: ホテルのメイン・ダイニング「ザ・レストラン」。昼食には数多くの前菜、デザートがビュッフェ形式で提供される。ロンドンのビジネス・エグゼクティブに好評なレストラン。**19,20**: 現在の二代目オーナーの名がつけられた「ザ・サンダーソン・スイート」。応接間、天蓋付きベッドを置いた主寝室、控室(写真20)、浴室で構成。

16–18: *The Restaurant*, the main dining room, is popular with London businessmen. A lavish buffet, with numerous hors d'oeuvres and desserts, is served at lunchtime. **19, 20**: *The Sanderson Suite* is named after the present, second-generation owner. It comprises a drawing room, bedroom with canopy bed, waiting room (shown in photo no. 20), and bathroom.

154 — Selsdon Park Hotel

24
25

21–23: 3つの部屋から成る「ファーリー・スイート」。**22**: 英国の伝統的朝食のひとつ、キッパーズ(ニシンの燻製)を取り入れたルーム・サービスのセッティング。ハドック(タラの燻製)も用意されている。**24, 25**: 新装されたスタンダードの部屋「シングル・ルーム」。なおホテル宿泊客には、敷地内のゴルフ場料金(18ホール、ワン・ラウンド)が割引きされる。ゴルフ場のオープン時間は、9時から10時半、14時半から16時まで、土曜日にはゴルフ・クリニックが催される。

●●●

21–23: The *Farleight Suite* is made up of three rooms. **22:** A traditional English breakfast setting from room service, featuring kippers. Haddock is also available. **24, 25:** A standard, newly redecorated *Single Room*. Hotel guests may also use the golf course on the grounds. The course is open from 9:00 to 10:30 a.m. and 2:30 to 4:00 p.m., and a golf clinic is held Saturdays.

Great Hotels of the World: vol. 4 —— 155

Hotel du Palais
1 Avenue de L'Imperatrice, 64200 Biarritz, France

　ナポレオン3世とウージェニー皇后の離宮がこのホテルの起源である。1854年、ウージェニーがスペインから嫁いできたことから、スペイン国境に近いフランス南西海岸のビアリッツに離宮が設けられ、1856年に完成した。"ヴィラ・ウージェニー"と名づけられ、皇后の頭文字を取ったユニークなE型平面のネオ・クラシック様式。建築家はE・クーヴルシェフ。第二帝政が終るまでの15年間、ビアリッツは欧州の王侯・貴族が集い遊ぶ避寒地として名を高めた。1903年2月2日、離宮は火災で損傷、建築家エドゥアール・ニエルマンにより1905年に再建された。第一次大戦の勃発で華麗なベル・エポックの時代は終り、離宮は一時、軍の病院として使われた。

　1952年に至って、ビアリッツ市が離宮を所有、内部の修復工事を行ない、ホテルとして運営されることになった。現在では、世界の上流階級が訪れる名門ホテルとして知られている。

●●●

The Hotel du Palais was originally an imperial villa used by Emperor Napoleon III and Empress Eugénie. It was built by Eugénie in the town of Biarritz, in southwest France near the Spanish border. Construction began in 1854 and was completed in 1856. The architect was Eugén Couvrechef, and the plan of the Neo-Classical "Villa Eugénie" was in the shape of the letter "E"—the Empress's initial. In the 15 years before the end of the Second Empire, Biarritz established itself as a winter resort for European royalty and aristocracy. The Villa was destroyed by fire in 1903, and was rebuilt in 1905 by architect Edouard Niermans.

With the outbreak of World War I, the glittering "Belle Epoque" was truly over, and the villa was temporarily used as a military hospital. In 1952 the villa, owned by the city of Biarritz, was restored and remodeled as a hotel. Today it has an excellent reputation as one of the world's top-class luxury hotels.

1,2: ビアリッツは18世紀後期から王族たちの保養地で、オルターンス皇后(皇妃ジョゼフィーヌの娘)やアングレーム公爵夫人(ルイ16世の娘)などが訪れた記録がある。現在のホテルは火災後、三階建に増築されたもの。3: 長年総支配人を務めるラインバッヒャー氏。4:「エントランス・ホール」奥に残されているクラシックな階段。階段裏に「レセプション」がある。

●●●

1, 2: Since the late 18th century Biarritz was a health resort for the royal families of Europe, and there are records of visits by Queen Hortense, daughter of Empress Josephine, and the Duchess of Angoulême, daughter of Louis XVI. The third floor of the present hotel was added after the fire 3: Jean-Louis Leimbacher has been General Manager for many years. 4: A classic staircase has been preserved in one corner of the *Entrance Hall*. Behind the stairway is the *Reception* desk.

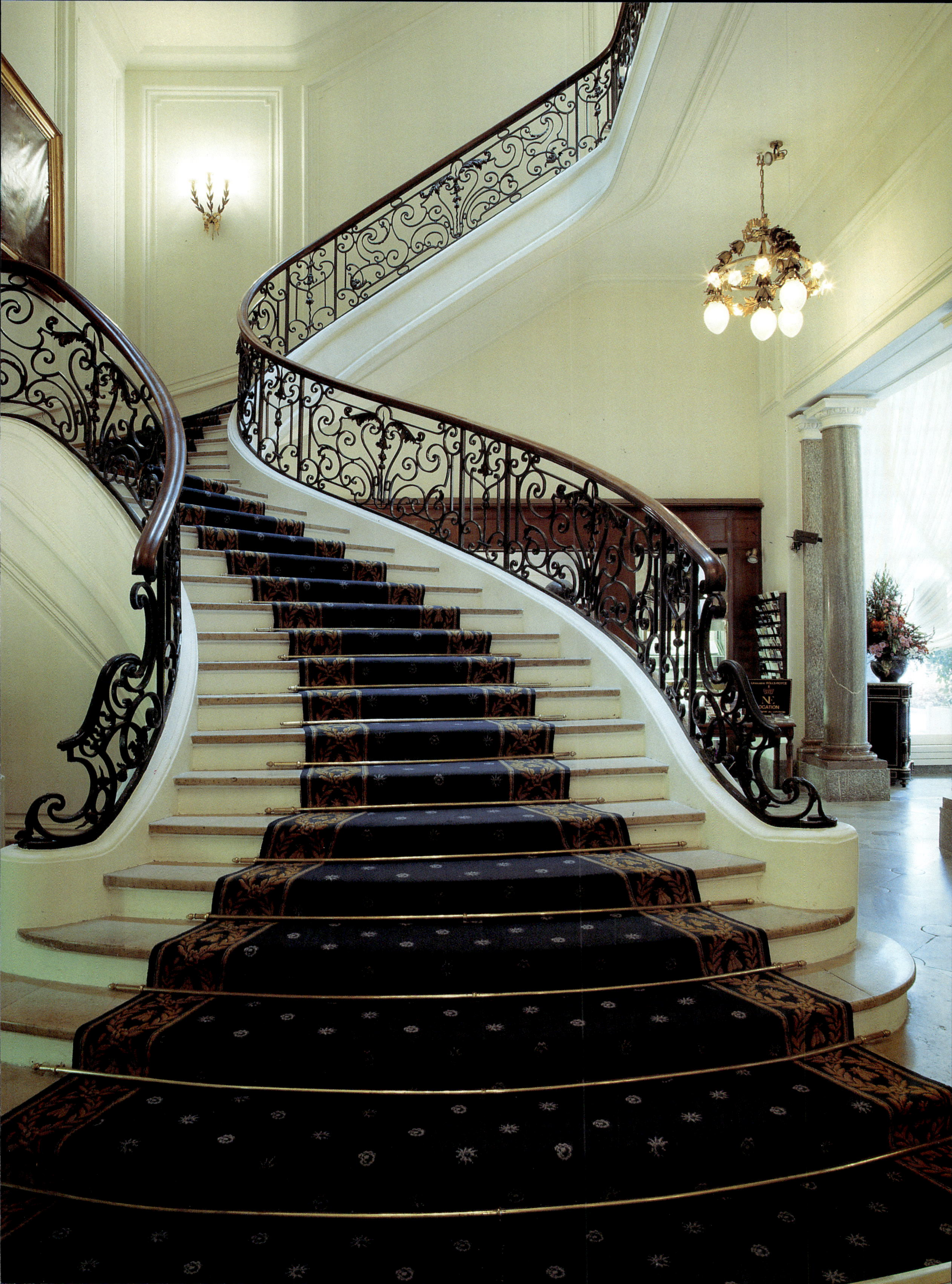

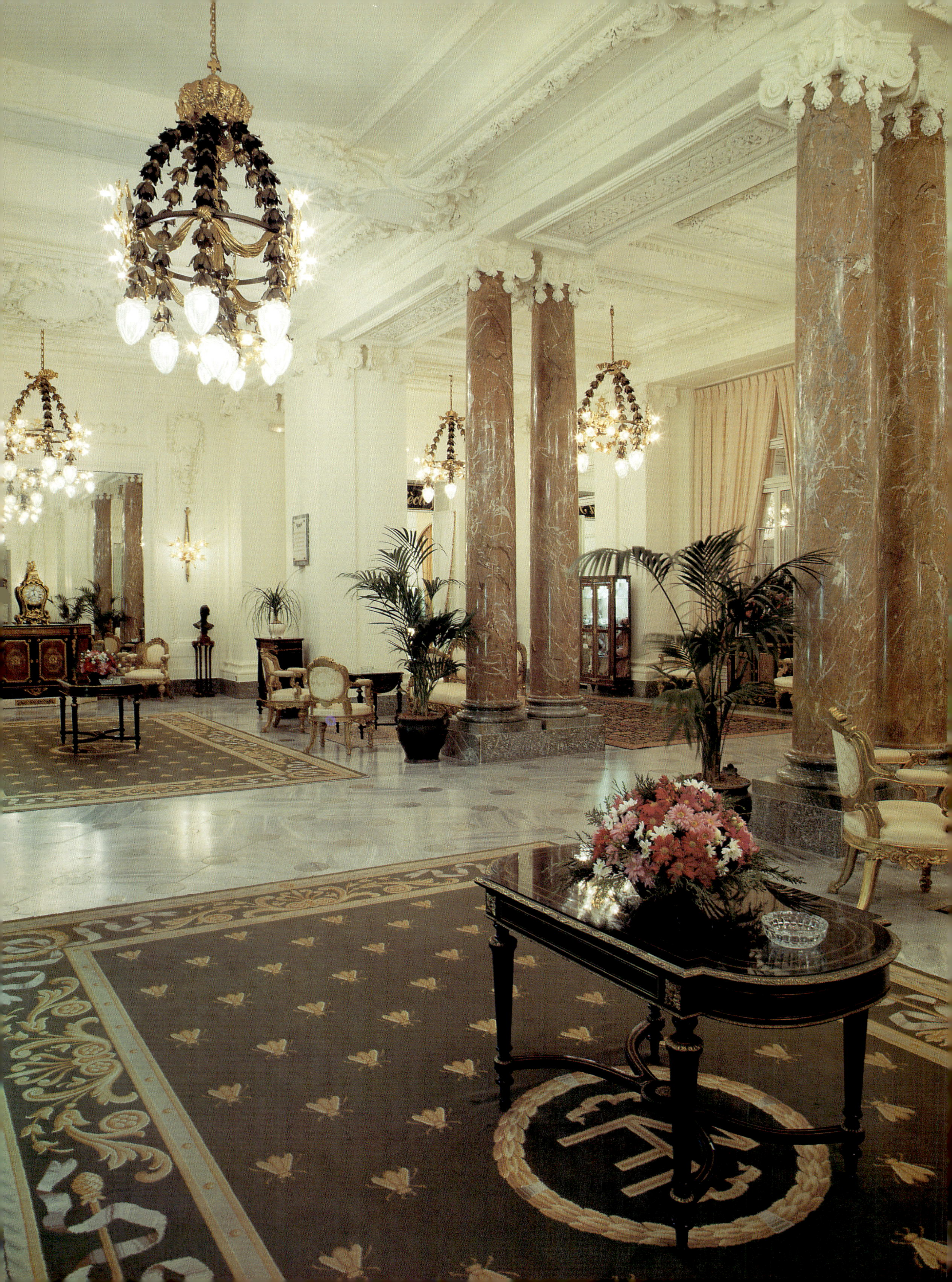

5-10: 入口の豪華な「エントランス・ホール」。蝉（セミ）の文様の絨毯、葡萄装飾のあるイオニア式柱頭、花びらが連なるシャンデリアなどは、再建時にアール・ヌーボー様式を取り入れてつくられた。シャンデリアや絨毯にはナポレオン3世とウージェニー皇后を表わすNEのロゴがデザインされている。家具の一部に火災を免れた19世紀のオリジナルが使われている。6, 10: 円形の「コンシェルジュ・デスク」。

●●●

5-10: The magnificent *Entrance Hall*. The cicada-patterned carpeting, Ionic columns with grapevine design, and the flower-petal chandeliers are all Art Nouveau touches from the time the villa was rebuilt. The chandeliers and carpeting incorporate a design using the letters "N-E", standing for Napoleon and Eugénie. Some of the furnishings are 19th-century originals that escaped the fire. 6, 10: The round *Concierge Desk*.

Great Hotels of the World: vol. 4 —— 159

11-13: 1860年に描かれたナポレオン3世とウージェニー皇后の肖像画が飾られている階段。階段下に、"ヴィラ・ウージェニー"の建築記録が表示されている。ウージェニーは、スペインのモンティホ伯爵の令嬢だった。14:「ビリヤード・ルーム」としても使われていた大宴会場「サロン・アンペリヤル」。火災後の再建時には天窓があったと思われる。15:「サロン・マチルド」。ホテルには計8ヶ所の宴会場と会議施設がある。

11-13: An 1860 portrait of Napoleon and Eugénie hangs over the stairway. A construction record for the "Villa Eugénie" is displayed at the foot of stairs. Eugénie was a daughter of Count Montijo in Spain. 14: The *Salon Imperial* is also used as a *Billiard Room*. The ceiling probably had skylights at the time of the building's reconstruction in 1905. 15: *Salon Methilde*, one of a total of eight banquet and meeting rooms.

160 —— Hotel du Palais

14
15

Great Hotels of the World: vol.4 —— 161

162 — Hotel du Palais

16-18:「エントランス・ホール」(左)と「ラ・ロトンド(円堂)」(右)の中間に設けられた「バー」。19-25: 200人を収容するメイン・ダイニング「ラ・ロトンド」は、大西洋を望む半円形のレストラン。円柱と壁を黄金のアンピール様式で飾っている。以前には半円形の天窓があった。屋根の部分は2階にある最高級の部屋専用のテラスになっている。24:「ラ・ロトンド」につながるグルメ・レストラン「ル・グラン・シエクル(大世紀)」30席。ここはもと虎の皮を敷いた「ザ・タイガー・ドローイング・ルーム」があったらしい。

16-18: The *Bar* is situated between the *Entrance Hall* (left) and *La Rotonde* restaurant (right). 19-25: The semi-circular main dining room, *La Rotonde*, seats 200 and offers a view of the Atlantic. The columns and walls are decorated in gold Empire style, and the ceiling once contained semi-circular skylights. A portion of the second floor is reserved for guests staying in top-class rooms. 24: *Le Grand Siècle*, a gourmet restaurant connected to *La Rotonde*, seats 30. This is believed to have originally been the *Tiger Drawing Room*, which was decorated with tiger skins.

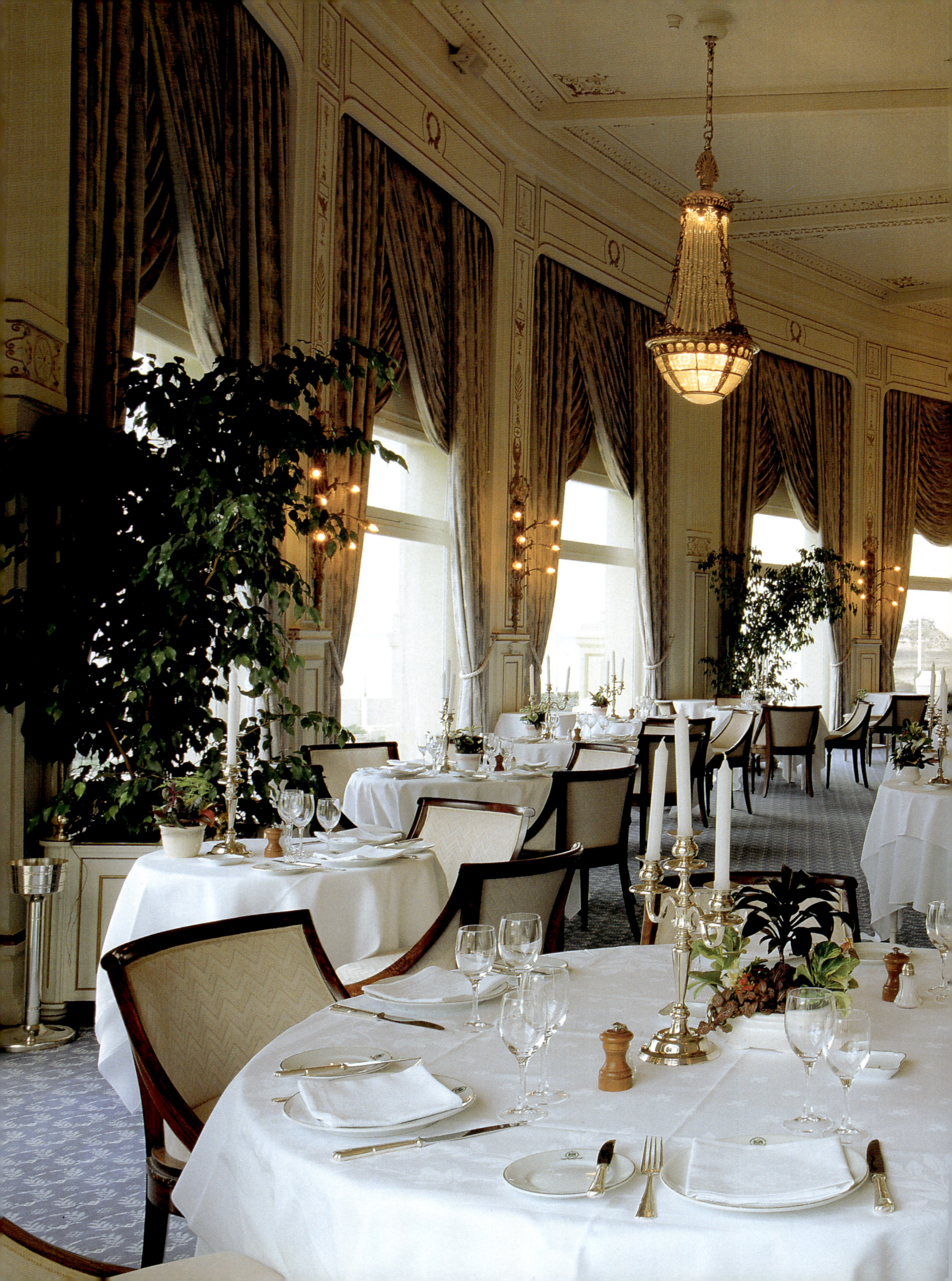

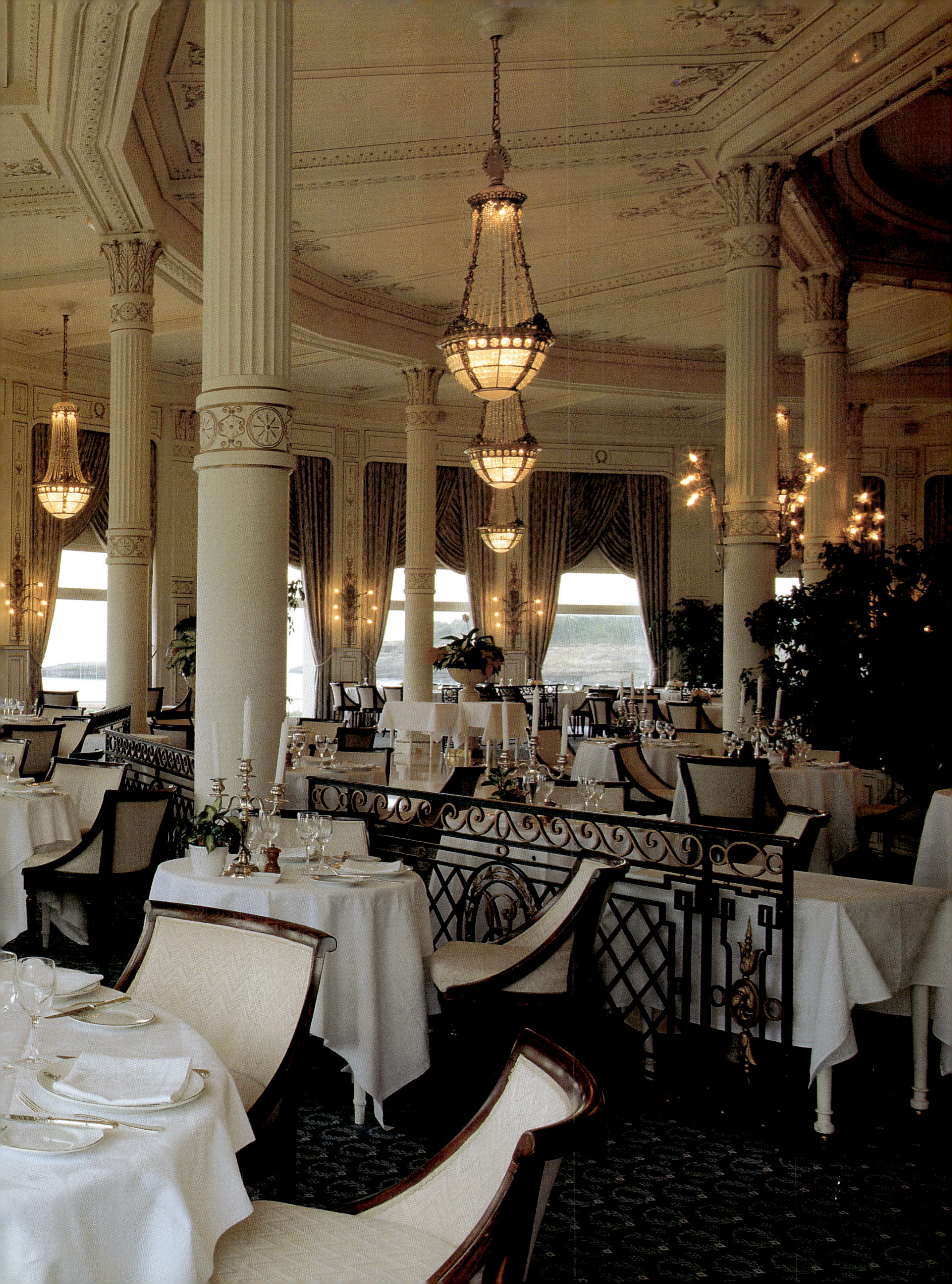

26
27
28
29
30

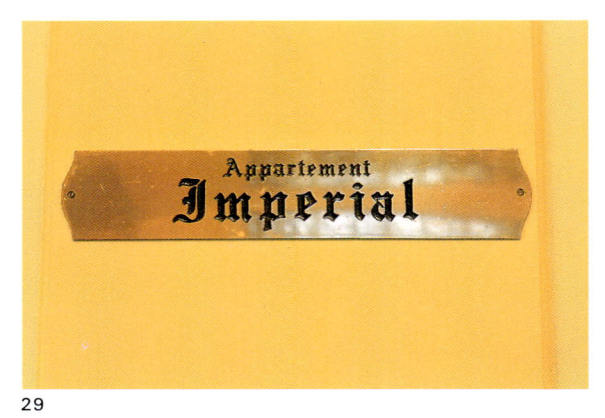

31

32

26-30: 控室、応接間、寝室、浴室で構成される最高級の部屋のひとつ「アパルトマン・アンペリヤル」。応接間にはルイ16世式の家具が置かれている。浴室の水道蛇口、王冠のロゴを付けたバス・タブなど、クラシックな雰囲気にコーディネイトされている。**31-32**: 壁上部にまで達するワードローブ用の踏台を備えた「スイート・ルーム」。20世紀初頭、長期滞在客のために特につくられた。

◆◆◆

26–30: The *Appartement Imperial*, a top-class suite, includes a drawing room with Louis XVI style furnishings, a waiting room, bedroom and bathroom. The bathroom water faucets, the crown design on the bathtub and other elements add to the classic air of the suite. **31–32**: A wardrobe, extending almost to the ceiling and equipped with a footstool, is part of this *Suite*, built in the early 20th century for long-term residential guests.

Great Hotels of the World: vol. 4 —— 167

168 —— Hotel du Palais

37
38

33-36: 3階に置かれている最高級の部屋のひとつ「アパルトマン・サラ・ベルナール」。ネオ・ロココ様式のアーム・チェアーが使われている。**34**: 窓の下方に見える石の手摺を付けたテラスがメイン・ダイニング「ラ・ロトンド」の屋上。**37, 38**: 英国王ジョージ5世の肖像写真を飾った英国調の「スイート・ルーム」。寝室のナイト・テーブル上のライトは灰皿をセットした独特なもの。英国王エドワード7世（在位1901〜10年）もこのホテルを好み、ヨーロッパ大陸最初のゴルフ・コースを隣接地にオープンさせた。世界で最も美しいホテルのひとつと評価されている。

33–36: The top-class *Appartement Sarah Bernhart* on the third floor is furnished with neo-Rococo armchairs. **34**: The terrace, with stone railings visible beneath the windows, is on the roof of *La Rotonde*. **37, 38**: A photographic portrait of England's King George V hangs in this English-style *Suite*. The unusual light over the bedroom night table has a built-in ashtray. Britain's King Edward VII, who reigned from 1901 to 1910, enjoyed visiting the hotel, and the first golf course in Continental Europe occupies an adjoining site. The hotel has a reputation as one of the most beautiful in the world.

Hotel du Louvre
Place André Malraux, 75001 Paris, France

　ホテル・デュ・ルーヴルは、パリで最初のグランド・ホテル（近代設備を導入した大型ホテル）といわれる。開業は1855年、室数800室。オスマンのパリ改造計画の一環であった。ルーヴル宮とオペラ座通りの間に位置する好立地から、歴史的な会議が数多く開催されることになる。

　1875年12月6日、このホテルのサロンで〝自由の女神像〟をアメリカに贈ろうという運動の最初の会議が開かれた。女神像を制作した彫刻家はバルトルディ。当時、女神像のミニチュアを販売するというアイデアを思いつき、資金集めに奮闘したガジェ氏を讃える意味で、ギャジット（Gadget＝装置、仕掛け、妙案の意）という新語が生まれたという。現在、インテリア・デザイナーのシビル・ド・マージョリーにより新感覚の内装を取り入れるリノヴェーションが進行している。

●●●

　The Hotel du Louvre is known as the first of Paris's "Grand Hotels" (as the new, large-scale hotels equipped with modern facilities came to be called). It opened in 1855 with 600 rooms, and was part of Haussmann's great reconstruction plan for Paris. With its choice location between the Palais du Louvre and the Avenue de l'Opéra, it was the site of numerous historic meetings.

　At one such meeting, in December 1875 in a salon of the hotel, the campaign to donate the Statue of Liberty to the United States got underway. According to the story the statue, designed by sculptor Frederic Bartholdi, needed funding, and a man named Mr. Gaget came up with the idea of selling miniature copies of the statue to raise funds. Since then the word "gadget," after Mr. Gaget, came to mean any special device used for accomplishing a goal. Interior designer Sybille De Margerie was responsible for the recent renovation of the interior.

1-3,6: 1927年に現在地に移転して再開業した由緒深いホテル。建築家はA・ペレシェー。旧ホテルは現ホテルの裏手の建物にあった。もとの名は〝グラン・オテル・デュ・ルーヴル〟。1855年の万国博覧会のためにナポレオン3世がペレール兄弟の出資で建設させた。1・2階に店舗を持つ800室の大ホテルだったという。4:「エントランス・ホール」の階段。ミロのヴィーナスのレプリカが置かれている。

●●●

1-3, 6: In 1927 this historic hotel reopened in its present location; A. Pellechet was the architect for the reconstruction. The original hotel, the Grand Hotel du Louvre, stood behind the present site. It was built by Emperor Napoleon III, with investment money from the Pereire brothers, for the World's Fair. It contained some 800 guest rooms, with stores on the first and second floors. 4: The *Entrance Hall* stairway, with a replica of the statue "Vénus de Milo."

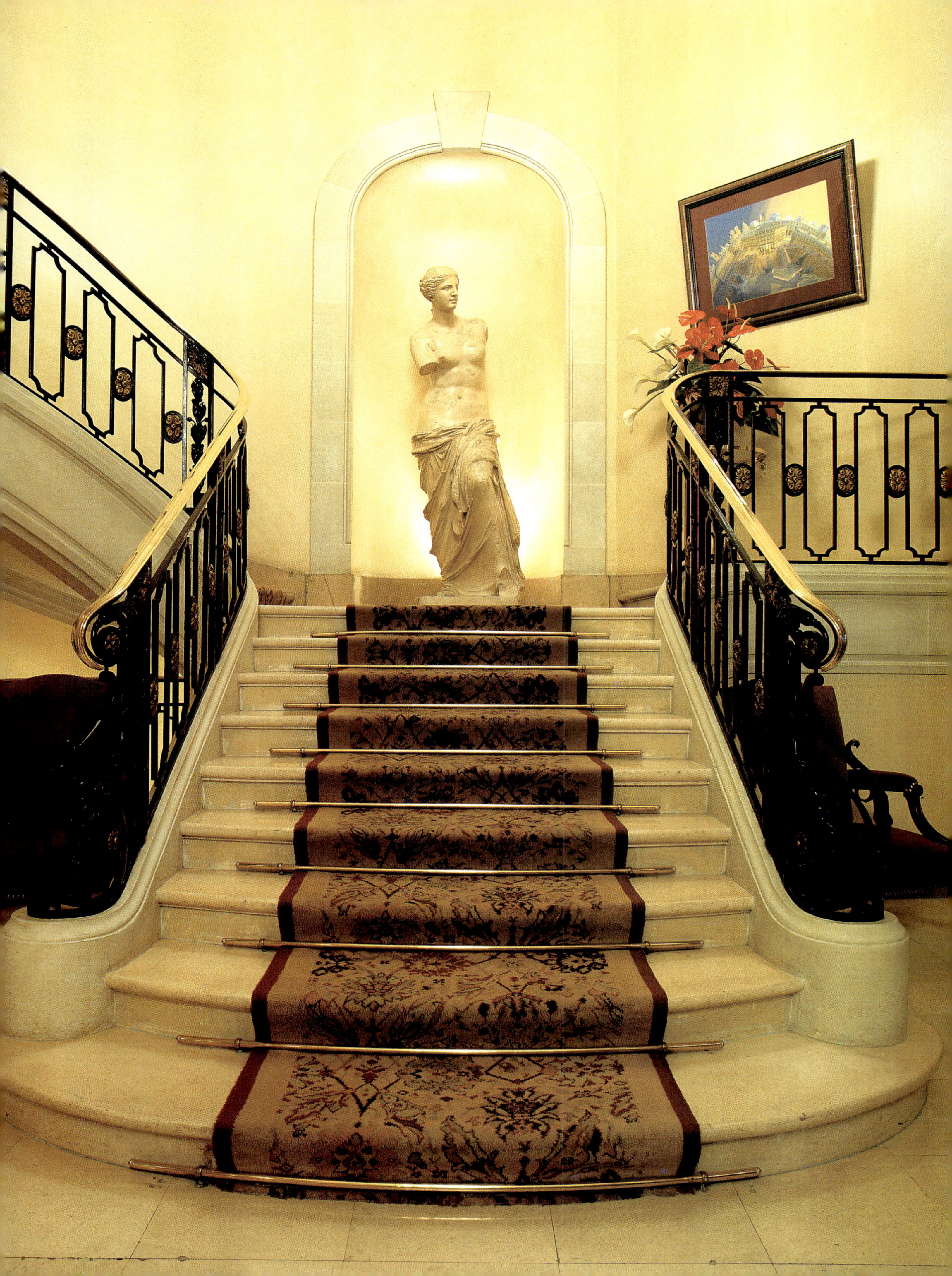

172——Hotel du Louvre

5,7,8:「エントランス・ホール」の「レセプション」。イオニア式円柱、クリスタル・シャンデリアで飾られ、中2階にホテル・オフィスがある。9〜11:「モナリザ」を意味するバー「ラ・ジョコンド」。お茶を楽しむラウンジでもある。

5, 7, 8: The *Entrance Hall*, with Ionic columns and a crystal chandelier, holds the *Reception* area. The hotel office is on the mezzanine level.
9–11: *La Joconde* bar (French for "Mona Lisa") also has a lounge which serves tea.

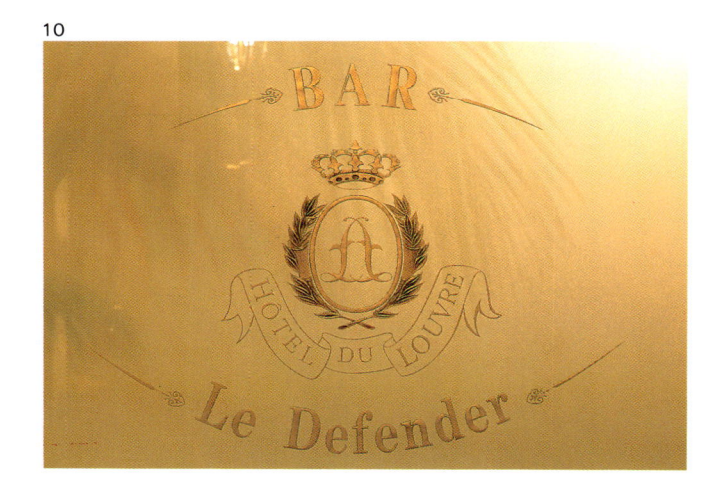

Great Hotels of the World: vol. 4 — 173

12

13

"Miss Liberty was born at the Hôtel du Louvre in Paris"
Collection et cliché, Bibliothèque du Conservatoire National des Arts et Métiers, Paris.

174———Hotel du Louvre

16

17

18

12-14：旧ホテルの大宴会場をイメージしてつくられたグランド・サロン「ロアン」。13：「自由の女神」像を誕生させた初会議の情景を描いた絵画。旧ホテルでのエピソード（イラスト提供：ホテル・デュ・ルーヴル）。15‐18：1990年3月にリノヴェーションを終えた「ブラスリー・デュ・ルーヴル」。ホテルの周辺を描いた数々の油絵が壁を飾っている。

12–14: *Le Grand Salon Rohan* recreates the ambience of the large banquet areas in the original hotel. 13: A painting showing the first meeting leading to the creation of the Statue of Liberty, in the original hotel. (Illustration courtesy of Hotel du Louvre). 15–18: Renovation work on *La Brasserie du Louvre* was completed in March 1990. Numerous oil paintings depicting the surrounding neighborhood hang from the walls.

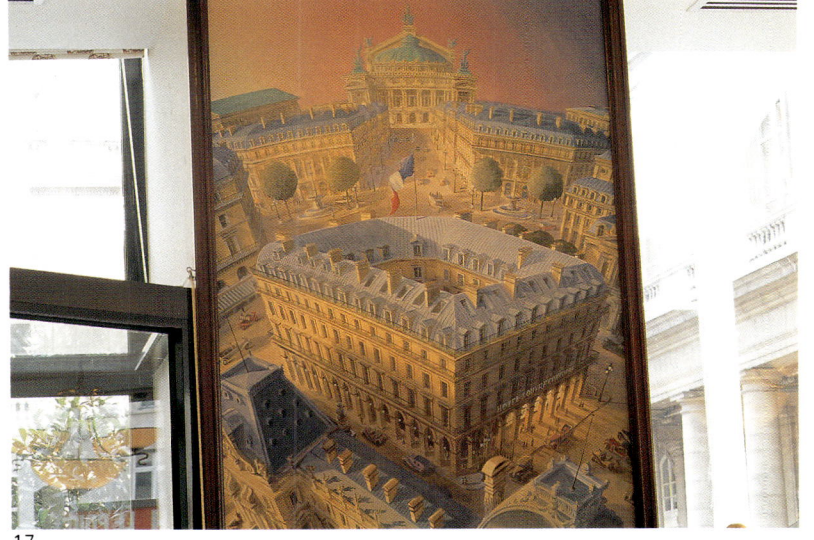

176——Hotel du Louvre

22

23

24

19–21: 浴室からもオペラ座を眺望できる5階に設けられた「スイート・ルーム」。22, 24: 黄色を基調としたスタンダードの「ツイン・ルーム」。オペラ座が見える部屋である。23: ブルーでコーディネイトされた「ジュニアー・スイート」。客室と「ブラスリー・デュ・ルーヴル」のリノヴェーションは、デザイナーのシビル・ド・マージョリーが担当した。

19–21: This fifth-floor *Suite* has a view of the Opera House from the bathroom. 22, 24: A standard *Twin Room*, decorated in yellow, with a view of the Opera House. 23: A *Junior Suite*, decorated in blue. Sybille De Margerie was responsible for redecoration of the guest rooms and *La Brasserie du Louvre*.

Great Hotels of the World: vol. 4 — 177

Hotel Concorde Saint-Lazare
108, Rue Saint-Lazare, 75008 Paris, France

　パリ万国博のシンボル・タワーとしてエッフェル塔が完成した1889年、パリにフランス最初の大型ステーション・ホテルが誕生した。オペラ座のサン・ラザール駅と同時に開発されたグランド・ホテル・テルミニュスで、開業は1889年5月1日。建築家はサン・ラザール駅の設計を手がけたジュスト・リッシュ。2階の高さに設けた渡り廊下で駅とホテルを結ぶ画期的な設計であった。ホテルとしては最初の蒸気動力式エレベーターも設置したが、客の好みに合わず、サービス用として使われた。

　開業時の部屋数は500室。全室が暖炉と次の間つきの設計で、内装はネオ・クラシカル様式、家具はルイ14世式で調えられた。ロビーの壁面を飾る天使像のうち、なぜか一体だけが後ろ向きに描かれ、客の話題となった。1956年にホテル・コンコルド・サン・ラザールと改称され、近年、内部のリノヴェーションが行なわれた。

The Grand Hotel Terminus, France's first large-scale station hotel, opened in 1889, the same year the Eiffel Tower was completed. It was connected to Saint-Lazare station, behind Paris's Opera House, by a unique two-story elevated passageway. Architect Juste Lisch was responsible for both the hotel and the station, which opened at the same time.

The world's first steam-powered elevators were installed, but since they weren't popular with guests they were used as service elevators. There were a total of 500 guest rooms, all with connecting doors to adjacent rooms and all equipped with heaters. Louis XIV furniture is used throughout the Neo-Classical rooms. The interior was recently renovated, along with the paintings of angels that cover the lobby walls. One of the angels is painted with its back turned, and this has often provided a topic of conversation among guests. The hotel was renamed the Hotel Concorde Saint-Lazare in 1956.

1,2：写真左がサン・ラザール駅。開業期のホテルは、駅のプラット・ホームから荷物なしで歩いて（駅のポーターが部屋まで運んでくれた）、チェック・インできた。3：2連鋳鉄円柱が残っている「セントラル・ホール」。「リーディング・ルーム」とも呼ばれていた。開業時にはここに大階段があって、渡り廊下で駅に結ばれていた。2・3階にあった「セントラル・ホール」を見下すギャラリーは現在はふさがれている。

1, 2: Saint-Lazare Station is visible on the left. When the hotel opened, guests could walk directly from the station platforms, without their luggage, to the hotel check-in; station porters would carry their luggage to their rooms. 3: The original coupled cast-iron columns remain in the *Central Hall*, once known as the *Reading Room*. There was originally a grand staircase here, leading to the station via the two-story passageway. A gallery overlooking the Central Hall, which extended over the second and third floors, is now closed.

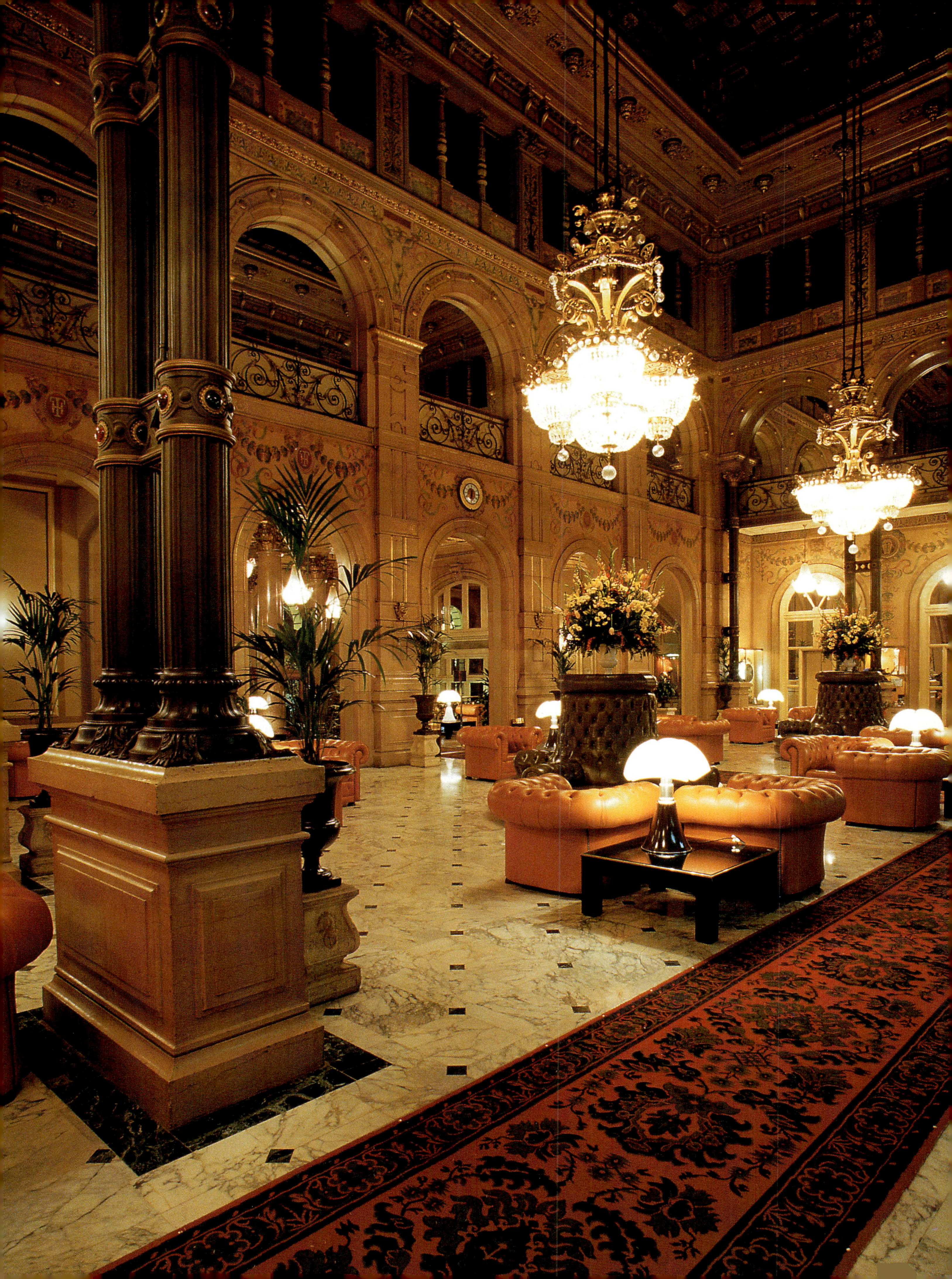

4

5

6

7

8

9

4：コリント式円柱で飾られた「エントランス・ホール」。5：「エントランス・ホール」階段上部左手の廊下奥に客室に通ずる階段が置かれている（写真19は反対方向から撮影）。6-9：旧ホテルの紋章H.T.（ホテル・テルミニュス）と、神秘的な"後姿の天使"が壁に描かれ、オリジナルな大クリスタル・シャンデリアで飾られた「セントラル・ホール」。10：駅とホテルを結んでいた渡り廊下。1940年に使用中止になった。11：開業期のホテル写真（写真提供：ホテル・コンコルド・サンラザール）。

●●●

4: Corinthian columns in the *Entrance Hall*. 5: At the top of the *Entrance Hall* staircase, at the end of the hallway to the left, is a stairway leading to the guest rooms. (Photo no. 19 shows the view from the opposite side). 6-9: The walls of the *Central Hall* are decorated with the former hotel crest, with the letters "H-T" (standing for Hotel Terminus), as well as the mysterious form of an angel seen from the back. The original large crystal chandeliers hang from the ceiling. 10: The passageway connecting the hotel with the station was used until 1940. 11: The hotel when it first opened. (Photo courtesy of Hotel Concorde Saint-Lazare).

10

11

Great Hotels of the World: vol. 4 — *181*

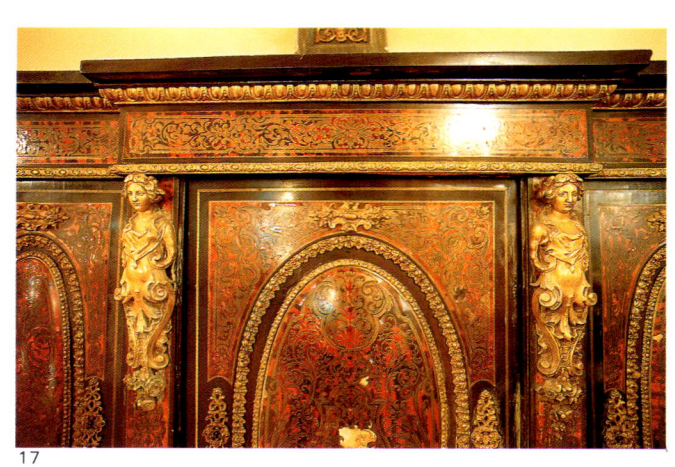

12,13：中2階には、4つの「コンフェランス・ルーム」がある。そのひとつ「サロン・アテン（アテネの間）」で催されたカクテル・パーティーのセッティング。14,15：アメリカン・バー「ル・ゴールデン・ブラック」。16,17,19：階段の踊り場を飾るアンティーク家具。18：ビリヤード台の上に照明ライトを吊ったクラシックな「ビリヤード・ルーム」。各台には、そこでビリヤードを楽しんだ世界の著名人の名札が付けられている。

12, 13: A cocktail party setting in the *Salon Athenes*, one of four *Conference Rooms* on the mezzanine level. 14, 15: *Le Golden Black*, an American-style bar. 16, 17, 19: Antique furnishings in a staircase landing. 18: Lighting fixtures hang above each table in the *Billiard Room*. The tables have nameplates with the names of famous people from around the world who played billiarcs.

182 —— Hotel Concorde Saint-Lazare

18
19

Great Hotels of the World: vol.4 —— 183

184——Hotel Concorde Saint-Lazare

23

24

20, 21:窓側と内側のセクションを持つレストラン「ル・カフェ・テルミニュス」。価値ある料理を提供するレストランとの評価が高い。**22**:「ル・カフェ・テルミニュス」の入口にある「ビストロ108」。ホテル客用の朝食レストランとしても使われている。**23, 24**:新装された「ツイン・ルーム」。コーナーにシッティング・スペースのあるブルーでコーディネイトされた細長い部屋。

20, 21: *Le Cafe Terminus*, with separate window and inside sections, has a reputation for high-quality food and good value. **22**: *Bistrot 108*, at the entrance to *Le Cafe Terminus*, serves breakfast to hotel guests. **23, 24**: A rectangular *Twin Room* with a corner sitting area, newly redecorated in blue.

Great Hotels of the World: vol. 4 — 185

25

26 27

Hotel Concorde Saint-Lazare

28

29

25-27：共布（ともぬの）のベッド・カバーとカーテンを用いた新装の「ツイン・ルーム」。新しい部屋のコーディネイトは若いインテリア・デザイナーのシビル・ド・マージョリーが担当。**28,29**：ホテルのコーナーに配した英国調の部屋「ツイン・スーピリア」。ルーム・サービスで運ばれた朝食のセッティング。開業時には、しばしばフランス印象派の画家モネ（1840-1926）がこのホテルで週末を過ごしたという。

●●●

25-27: A *Twin Room* with matching curtains and bedcovers. Interior coordination was handled by young interior designer Sybille De Margerie. **28, 29**: A room service breakfast setting in an English-style, corner *Twin Superior* room. The French Impressionist painter Claude Monet (1840–1926) reportedly spent many weekends in the hotel in its early days.

Hotels List

The Peninsula, Hong Kong
Salisbury Road, Kowloon, Hong Kong
Tel:366-6251 Fax:722-4170 Telex:43821
Summary of hotel facilities
Total guest rooms:210 (including 20 suites)
Restaurants: 3
Bars, lounges: 3
Banquet rooms: 1
施設概要
総客室数:210室(20スイート)
レストラン:3ヵ所
バー、ラウンジ:3ヵ所
宴会施設:1ヵ所
その他:ショッピング・アーケード
日本事務所
ザ ペニンシュラ グループ
100東京都千代田区有楽町1-5-2
　　東宝ツインタワービル6階
Tel:(03)3595-8084 Fax:(03)3502-2467

Mandarin Oriental, Hong Kong
5 Connaught Road, Central, Hong Kong
Tel:522-0111 Fax:810-6190 Telex:73653
Summary of hotel facilities
Total guest rooms: 547 (including 58 suites)
Restaurants: 4
Bars, lounges: 4
Banquet rooms: 6
施設概要
総客室数:547室(58スイート)
レストラン:4ヵ所
バー、ラウンジ:4ヵ所
宴会施設:6ヵ所
その他:屋内プール、ヘルス・クラブ
日本事務所
マンダリン・オリエンタル・ホテル・グループ
105東京都港区新橋6-3-5 アタゴ小林ビル3階
Tel:(03)3433-3388 Fax:(03)3433-3347

The Regent Hong Kong
Salisbury Road, Kowloon, Hong Kong
Tel: 721-1211 Fax: 739-4546
Telex:HX37134
Summary of hotel facilities
Total guest rooms:602 (including 70 suites)
Restaurants: 3
Bars, lounges: 2
Banquet rooms: 9
施設概要
総客室数:602室(70スイート)
レストラン:3ヵ所
バー、ラウンジ:2ヵ所
宴会施設:9ヵ所
その他:屋外プール2ヵ所
日本事務所
リージェント・インターナショナル・ホテル日本支社
100東京都千代田区有楽町1-10-1 有楽町ビル70
Tel:(03)3211-4541 Fax:(03)3211-4538

Island Shangri-La Hong Kong
Pacific Place, 88 Queensway, Central,
Hong Kong
Tel:877-3838 Fax:521-8742
Telex:70373 ISLP HX
Summary of hote facilities
Total guest rooms: 566 (including 34 suites)
Restaurants: 5
Bars, lounges: 4
Banquet rooms: 6
施設概要
総客室数:566室(34スイート)
レストラン:5ヵ所
バー、ラウンジ:4ヵ所
宴会施設:6ヵ所
その他:屋外プール
日本事務所
シャングリラ インターナショナル日本支社
103東京都中央区日本橋小網町14-1 日新ビル6階
Tel:(03)3667-7744 Fax:(03)3667-7743

The Oriental, Singapore
5 Raffles Avenue,
Marina Square, Singapore 0103
Tel:(65)339-0066 Fax:(65)339-9537
Telex:29117
Summary of hotel facilities
Total guest rooms:515 (including 100 suites)
Restaurants: 4
Bars, lounges: 4
Banquet rooms: 4
施設概要
総客室数:515室(100スイート)
レストラン:4ヵ所
バー、ラウンジ:4ヵ所
宴会施設:4ヵ所
その他:屋外プール
日本事務所
マンダリン・オリエンタル・ホテル・グループ
105東京都港区新橋6-3-5 アタゴ小林ビル3階
Tel:(03)3433-3388 Fax:(03)3433-3347

Shangri-La Hotel Singapore
Orange Grove Road, Singapore 1025
Tel:737-3644 Fax: 733-7220,1029
Telex:RS 21505
Summary of hotel facilities
Total guest rooms: 809 (including 58 suites)
Restaurants: 5
Bars, lounges: 3
Banquet rooms: 21
施設概要
総客室数:809室(58スイート)
レストラン:5ヵ所
バー、ラウンジ:3ヵ所
宴会施設:21ヵ所
その他:ミニ・ゴルフ場、ヘルスクラブ
日本事務所
シャングリラ インターナショナル日本支社
103東京都中央区日本橋小網町14-1 日新ビル6階
Tel: (03) 3667-7744 Fax: (03) 3667-7743

Hotel Inter·Continental Sydney
117 Macquarie Street, Sydney,
New South Wales, 2000 Australia
Tel:(02)230-0200 Fax:(02)251-2342
Telex:AA176890 IHCSYD
Summary of hotel facilities
Total guest rooms: 530 (including 42 suites)
Restaurants: 3
Bars, lounges: 3
Banquet rooms: 6
施設概要
総客室数:530室(42スイート)
レストラン:3ヵ所
バー、ラウンジ:3ヵ所
宴会施設:6ヵ所
その他:最上階屋内プール
日本事務所
インターコンチネンタルホテルズジャパン㈱
106東京都港区東麻布1-7-3 第2渡辺ビル7階
Tel:(03)5561-0701 Fax:(03)5561-0722
（フリーダイアル）0120-455655

The Dubai International Hotel
P.O.Box 10001, Dubai, U.A.E.
Tel:(4)245-111 Fax:(4)246-438
Telex:47333
Summary of hotel facilities
Total guest rooms: 354 (including 20 suites)
Restaurants: 3
Bars, lounges: 3
Banquet rooms: 8
施設概要
総客室数:354室(20スイート)
レストラン:3ヵ所
バー、ラウンジ:3ヵ所
宴会施設:8ヵ所
その他:ディスコ
日本事務所
ザ・リーディングホテルズ・オブ・ザ・ワールド日本支社
150東京都渋谷区渋谷2-17-3
Tel:(03)3797-3631 Fax:(03)3797-6701

Athens Ledra Marriott Hotel
115 Syngrou Avenue, Athens 117 45, Greece
Tel:(1)934-7711 Fax:(1)935-8603
Telex:223465 MARGR
Summary of hotel facilities
Total guest rooms: 258(including 16 suites)
Restaurants: 3
Bars, lounges: 3
Banquet rooms: 1
施設概要
総客室数:258室(16スイート)
レストラン:3ヵ所
バー、ラウンジ:3ヵ所
宴会施設:1ヵ所
その他:屋上プール
日本事務所
マリオット ホテル・リゾート&スイート日本支社
100東京都千代田区丸ノ内3-1-1 国際ビルB159
Tel:(03)3215-7258 （団体・営業予約）
Tel:(03)3215-7285 （個人予約）
Fax:(03)3215-7290
フリーダイアル(東京23区以外)0120-142536

Hotel La Mamounia
Avenue Bab Jdid, Marrakech, Morocco
Tal:(04)48981 Fax:(04)44940
Telex:72018
Summary of hotel facilities
Total guest rooms: 230 (including 50 suites)
Restaurants: 6
Bars, lounges: 6
Banquet rooms: 2
施設概要
総客室数:230室(50スイート)
レストラン:6ヵ所
バー、ラウンジ:6ヵ所
宴会施設:2ヵ所
その他:カジノ、ナイト・クラブ、ブティック、屋外プール、
テニス・コート
日本事務所
コンコルド ホテルズ
104東京都中央区築地4-1-1 東劇ビル6階
Tel:(03)3545-9571 Fax:(03)3545-9573

Hotel Palais Jamai
Bab El Guissa, Fez, Morocco
Tel:(06)343-31 Fax:(06)350-96
Telex:51974/51977
Summary of hotel facilities
Total guest rooms:131(including 10 suites)
Restaurants: 2
Bars, lounges: 1
Banquet rooms: 5
施設概要
総客室数:131室(10スイート)
レストラン:2ヵ所
バー、ラウンジ:1ヵ所
宴会施設:5ヵ所
その他:屋外プール、テニス・コート
日本事務所
104東京都中央区築地4-1-1 東劇ビル6階
Tel:(03)3545-9571 Fax:(03)3545-9573

Hotel Byblos Andaluz
Mi jas Golf, Mijas, Apt. 138 Fuengirola,
Malaga, Spain
Tel:52-473050 Fax:52-476783
Telex:79713
Summary of hotel facilities
Total guest rooms: 171 (including 54 suites)
Restaurants: 2
Bars, lounges: 3
Banquet rooms: 6
施設概要
総客室数:171室(54スイート)
レストラン:2ヵ所
バー、ラウンジ:3ヵ所
宴会施設:6ヵ所
その他:36ホール・ゴルフ場、ボディ・トリートメント施設、
屋外プール
日本事務所
コンコルド ホテルズ
104東京都中央区築地4-1-1 東劇ビル6階
Tel:(03)3545-9571 Fax:(03)3545-9573

Ambasciatori Palace Hotel
Via, V.Veneto 70, 00187 Rome, Italy
Tel:(06)47493 Fax:(06)4743601
Telex:610241
Summary of hotel facilities
Total guest rooms: 164 (including 14 suites)
Restaurants: 2
Bars, lounges: 2
Banquet rooms: 8
施設概要
総客室数:164室(14スイート)
レストラン:2ヵ所
バー、ラウンジ:2ヵ所
宴会施設:8ヵ所
その他:ビューティ・センター
日本事務所
コンコルド ホテルズ
104東京都中央区築地4-1-1 東劇ビル6階
Tel:(03)3545-9571 Fax:(03)3545-9573

Hotel Metropole Genève
34, quai General Guisan
CH-1204 Geneva, Switzerland
Tel:(022)21-13-44 Fax:(022)21-13-50
Telex:421550
Summary of hotel facilities
Total guest rooms: 145 (including 6 suites)
Restaurants: 2
Bars, lounges: 3
Banquet rooms: 5
施設概要
総客室数:145室(6スイート)
レストラン:2ヵ所
バー、ラウンジ:3ヵ所
宴会施設:5ヵ所
その他:屋上テラス
日本事務所
コンコルド ホテルズ
104東京都中央区築地4-1-1 東劇ビル6階
Tel:(03)3545-9571 Fax:(03)3545-9573

Atlantic Hotel, Kempinski Hamburg
An der Alster 72,
D-2000 Hamburg 1, Germany
Tel:(040)28-88-0 Fax:(040)24-71-29
Telex:2163297
Summary of hotel facilities
Total guest rooms: 278 (including 13 suites)
Restaurants: 3
Bars, lounges: 2
Banquet rooms: 15
施設概要
総客室数:278室(13スイート)
レストラン:3ヵ所
バー、ラウンジ:2ヵ所
宴会施設:15ヵ所
その他:屋内プール
日本事務所
ザ・リーディングホテルズ・オブ・ザ・ワールド日本支社
150東京都渋谷区渋谷2-17-3
Tel:(03)3797-3631 Fax:(03)3797-6701

Hotel Metropole Brussels
31, place de Brouckere,
B-1000 Brussels, Belgium
Tel:(2)217-23-00 Fax:(2)218-02-20
Telex:21234
Summary of hotel facilities
Total guest rooms: 410 (including 10 suites)
Restaurants: 2
Bars, lounges: 2
Banquet rooms: 7
施設概要
総客室数:410室(10スイート)
レストラン:2ヵ所
バー、ラウンジ:2ヵ所
宴会施設:7ヵ所
その他
日本事務所
コンコルド　ホテルズ
104東京都中央区築地4-1-1　東劇ビル6階
Tel:(03)3545-9571　Fax:(03)3545-9573

Selsdon Park Hotel
Sanderstead, South Croydon,
Surrey, CR2 8YA, U. K.
Tel:(081)657-8811 Fax:(081)651-6171
Telex:945003
Summary of hotel facilities
Total guest rooms:170 (including 7 suites)
Restaurants: 2
Bars, lounges: 2
Banquet rooms: 15
施設概要
総客室数:170室(7スイート)
レストラン:2ヵ所
バー、ラウンジ:2ヵ所
宴会施設:15ヵ所
その他:屋内プール、18ホール・ゴルフ場
日本事務所
コンコルド　ホテルズ
104東京都中央区築地4-1-1　東劇ビル6階
Tel:(03)3545-9571　Fax:(03)3545-9573

Hotel du Palais
1 Avenue de L'Impératrice,
64200 Biarritz, France
Tel:(33)59-24-09-40
Fax:(33)59-24-36-84
Telex:570000
Summary of hotel facilities
Total guest rooms: (138 including 20 suites)
Restaurants: 3
Bars, lounges: 1
Banquet rooms: 8
施設概要
総客室数:138室(20スイート)
レストラン:3ヵ所
バー、ラウンジ:1ヵ所
宴会施設:8ヵ所
その他:屋外プール
日本事務所
コンコルド　ホテルズ
104東京都中央区築地4-1-1　東劇ビル6階
Tel:(03)3545-9571　Fax:(03)3545-9573

Hotel du Louvre
Place André Malraux, 75001 Paris, France
Tel:(1) 42-61-56-01
Fax:(1) 42-60-02-90
Telex:220412
Summary of hotel facilities
Total guest rooms: 200 (including 15 suites)
Restaurants: 1
Bars, lounges: 1
Banquet rooms: 1
施設概要
総客室数:200室(15スイート)
レストラン:1ヵ所
バー、ラウンジ:1ヵ所
宴会施設:1ヵ所
日本事務所
コンコルド　ホテルズ
104東京都中央区築地4-1-1　東劇ビル6階
Tel:(03)3545-9571　Fax:(03)3545-9573

Hotel Concorde Saint-Lazare
108, rue Saint-Lazare, 75008 Paris, France
Tel:(1)40-08-44-44
Fax:(1)42-93-01-20
Telex:650442F
Summary of hotel facilities
Total guest rooms: 311 (including 15 suites)
Restaurants: 2
Bars, lounges: 1
Banquet rooms: 9
施設概要
総客室数:311室(15スイート)
レストラン:2ヵ所
バー、ラウンジ:1ヵ所
宴会施設:9ヵ所
その他:ビリヤード・ルーム
日本事務所
コンコルド　ホテルズ
104東京都中央区築地4-1-1　東劇ビル6階
Tel:(03)3545-9571　Fax(03)3545-9573

Profile

岸川惠俊

1951年、北海道小樽市に生まれる。1972年より、ワールド・カップ・スキー・レース、国際自動車ラリーの記録映画、TV番組などのムービー・カメラマンとして世界を廻る。1982年より、フォト・ジャーナリストに転向。以来、ライフワークとして、世界のホテル取材を開始する。年6ヵ月を海外取材に費し、1990年11月現在までに、世界の一流ホテル200ヵ所の取材を終える。日本商工会議所「石垣」(87-90)、柴田書店「ホテル・旅館」、プレジデント・クラブ「ステイタス」などの月刊誌に連載ページをもつ。企業ポスター、カレンダーなどの広告メディアにも、多くの写真を提供。1987年度、日野自動車カレンダー・世界の窓シリーズで全国カレンダー展入賞。

Hiro Kishikawa

Hiro Kishikawa was born in 1951 on Japan's northernmost island of Hokkaido. In 1972 he began working as a cameraman, traveling around the world covering World Cup ski races, international auto rallies and similar events. In 1982 he switched to photography, specializing in international hotels, and by November 1990, after traveling six months of each year, he had completed photo studies of some 200 first-class hotels around the world. He is a regular contributor to several monthly trade magazines in Japan, and has also provided many photographs for posters, calendars and other advertising media, including a 1987 calendar that won a prize in a Japanese nationwide calendar competition.

桐敷真次郎

1926年、東京都生まれ。1950年、東京大学工学部建築学科卒業。同大学院、ロンドン大学コートオールド美術研究所研究生を経て、1959年、一級建築士。1960年、東京都立大学工学部建築工学科助教授。1962年、工学博士。1971年、東京都立大学教授。1990年、東京家政学院大学教授。『建築学大系5・西洋建築史』『明治の建築』『建築史』『パラーディオ「建築四書」注解』等、著書・論文多数。1987年度日本建築学会賞(論文賞)受賞。第10回マルコ・ポーロ賞受賞。

Shinjiro Kirishiki

Born in Tokyo in 1926, Shinjiro Kirishki graduated from Department of Architecture, University of Tokyo in 1950. After studying as a graduate student of University of Tokyo and as a research student of University of London, he was registered architect in 1959 and was appointed Associate Professor of Architectural History, Department of Architecture, Tokyo Metropolitan University in 1960. In 1962 he was conferred D.Eng. from University of Tokyo. Since 1971, he was Professor of Architectural History and Design of the same university and an active member of the Architectural Institute of Japan. Professor Kirishiki is the author of "Architectural History," "Architecture of Meiji Period," "Commentary on Palladio's Four Books of Architecture," and many other books, papers and articles. He was awarded the 1986 Thesis Prize of the Architectural Institute of Japan and also the 10th Marco Polo Prize from the Istituto Italiano di Cultura in 1987. In 1990, he became Professor Emeritus of Tokyo Metropolitan University and Professor of Tokyo Kasei Gakuin University.

GREAT HOTELS OF THE WORLD: VOL.4
URBAN HOTEL FROM ASIA TO EUROPE

初版印刷	1991年9月15日
初版発行	1991年9月31日
写真・文	岸川惠俊
監修	桐敷真次郎
デザイン	北澤敏彦＋株式会社ディス・ハウス
翻訳	ロブ・サターホワイト
発行者	清水 勝
発行所	河出書房新社
	〒151 東京都渋谷区千駄ヶ谷2-32-2
	電話：(営業)03-3404-1201/(編集)03-3404-8611
	振替：東京0-10802
印刷	大日本印刷株式会社
製本	大口製本印刷株式会社

Copyright © Kawade Shobo Shinsha Publishers Ltd, #1991
Photography & Text copyright © Hiro Kishikawa 1991

本書からの二次使用(転載)は、著作権者の許可を必要とします。
また、コンピューター・ソフトへの写真入力使用、写真のトリミング使用、
写真の機械・電子的使用、フォトコピー、本書の録音など、
本書からの無断使用を禁じます。

落丁本、乱丁本はお取り替えします。
定価は帯・カバーに表示してあります。

ISBN4-309-71584-2

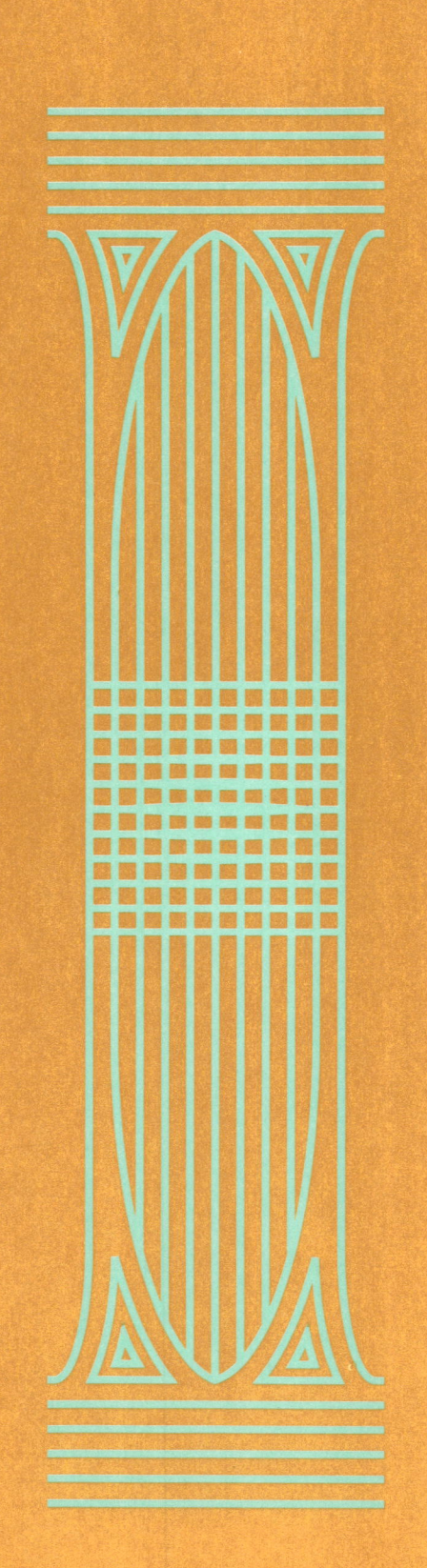

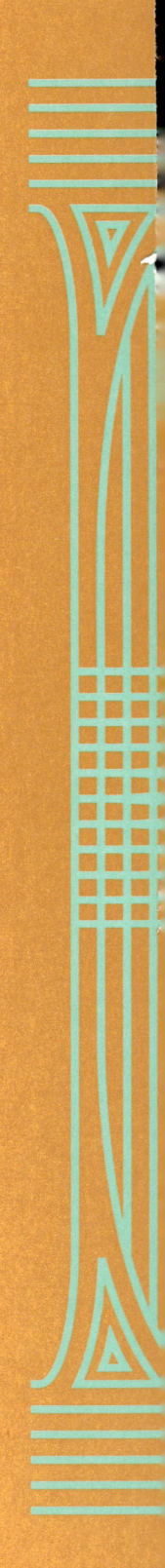